# Trauma Informed Support and Supervision for Those Working with Children at Risk



Working with at-risk children and their families is trauma-laden in nature, making exposure to occupational trauma a professional inevitability.

Child protection systems around the world have consistently been found to struggle with providing adequate quality supervision to practitioners within their workforce, leading to high rates of practitioner turnover. This book has been written in response to the lack of trauma-informed supervision models designed to support practitioners working in trauma-laden environments. It introduces professionals to the Trauma-Informed Support and Supervision (TISS) model, including all the elements that underpin the framework. Readers will be guided through a series of activities throughout the book preparing them to design and implement their own TISS plan in their own occupational setting. Case studies and vignettes are included as teaching tools within chapters. Catering to both frontline practitioners and line supervisors and managers, the TISS model normalises the experience of occupational traumatic stress and offers a preventative model of care and support as well as a guide to support practitioners post-exposure.

It will be of interest to all professionals who work with at-risk children and their families, including social workers, psychologists, nurses, healthcare professionals, teachers and other education professionals, counsellors, youth justice workers, lawyers and paralegals, family support and domestic and family violence practitioners, housing and homelessness workers as well as programme delivery professionals.

**Fiona Oates**, PhD, is a social work-trained practitioner, consultant, researcher and educator with more than 20 years of experience working with vulnerable children and their families. Dr Oates has a strong interest in supporting the professional development and wellbeing needs of practitioners working in trauma-laden environments with an emphasis on child protection. Dr Oates has developed a model of support that is trauma-informed and practitioner-centred: the TISS model. The TISS model acknowledges the challenging occupational environment that practitioners who support vulnerable children work in and has context-specific strategies embedded within to effectively support them. Dr Oates is based in Far North Queensland, Australia.

# Trauma Informed Support and Supervision for Those Working with Children at Risk

## Implementing the TISS Model in Practice

Fiona Oates

Routledge
Taylor & Francis Group
LONDON AND NEW YORK

Designed cover image: Getty Images

First published 2026
by Routledge
4 Park Square, Milton Park, Abingdon, Oxon OX14 4RN

and by Routledge
605 Third Avenue, New York, NY 10158

*Routledge is an imprint of the Taylor & Francis Group, an informa business*



*British Library Cataloguing-in-Publication Data*
A catalogue record for this book is available from the British Library

ISBN: 978-1-032-84861-7 (hbk)
ISBN: 978-1-032-84215-8 (pbk)
ISBN: 978-1-003-51537-1 (ebk)

DOI: 10.4324/9781003515371

Typeset in Sabon
by Apex CoVantage, LLC

This book is dedicated to those individuals who work tirelessly to support at-risk children and their families in the most challenging of environments.

You are important and you matter.

# Contents

# Preface

Working with at-risk children and their families is as rewarding as it is challenging. I began my career as a social worker in statutory child protection 22 years ago. Like many, I 'fell' into it. My fourth-year undergraduate social work placement had me working in the area of foster care assessments alongside a very experienced social worker. The unit was within a statutory child protection agency. At the end of my 14-week placement, I accepted a locum position in the child protection case work team to get some money together and to decide what I wanted to do next. Ten years later, I was still there. It was a challenging role in a deeply flawed system. However, what I found was that there were people like me who wanted to make a difference. Many coming from challenging backgrounds themselves. A group of practitioners with whom I felt a kinship. I found a deep sense of belonging. A vocation that I loved. A community of sorts. Until it wasn't. Once I started to struggle with symptomologies of occupational traumatic stress, I felt dislocated from that sense of belonging and community. From the vocation I adored. Unfortunately, my story is not an isolated one.

I have the deepest respect for practitioners who undertake work in at-risk children and their families across all practice settings. The ability to navigate the grey areas of life is a prerequisite of working in the field. To sit with some of the most heinous things humans can do to other humans. To feel the despair of multi-system failures that often create the conditions for child abuse and neglect to thrive. To witness the most horrific and unjust stories of violence, oppression, and trauma. The occupational environment is saturated with violence. Externally and often internally. Culturally, organisations that deliver services to at-risk children and their families struggle to provide effective support and supervision to their workforce. There are unwritten rules around the disclosure of struggles with occupational traumatic stress symptomologies, with many practitioners choosing not to seek support when they start to experience challenging occupational traumatic stress symptomologies for fear of negative impacts on their career.

As practitioners who work daily with people who have experienced trauma, we accept that brains are not meant to experience ongoing traumatic events. We know that without specialised intervention, problematic symptomologies can develop, which over time can be difficult to resolve. However, this understanding is rarely afforded to ourselves as practitioners. At-risk children and their families need skilled and knowledgeable practitioners who can assist them in navigating challenges so that they can best attend to the care and protection needs of their children. At-risk children and their families require practitioners who have the appropriate level of supervision and support that is responsive to their individual needs and that recognises the uniqueness of the role including the systems that create the environments they work in. At-risk children and their families need practitioners who are trained to care for them when they start to struggle with the inevitable symptomologies that can result from exposure to occupational traumatic stress. Practitioners who are supported and cared for are central to protecting children and strengthening families. That is why I developed the TISS model.

# Introduction

## Establishing the authority to speak: introduction to the author

I would like to begin our time together by sharing some of my story. Not long before writing this book, I attended a workshop about giving workshops – the presenter said that the most effective communicators of information are those who establish their authority to speak on the topic being discussed. They said that this lets the audience feel like they are in learned hands, allowing them to interact with the content more easily. This struck me as so simple but also so accurate. So to start, I would like to establish my authority to speak on the topic of occupational trauma exposure, its symptomology and strategies to manage them. I qualified as a social worker in 2003. The first ten years of my career I spent working in statutory child protection in regional parts of Australia.

During my time working in statutory child protection, I conducted interviews with children who had experienced physical and sexual abuse as well as emotional harm and neglect. At times, the bodies of these children were bruised, burnt, scarred, and unwashed. They told me details of what was happening in their lives with both their words and their behaviour. They told me their stories in police stations, in government cars, in sterile offices, in the principal's office at their school, in parks, in hospitals. Conducting assessments necessitated the reading of medical and police reports including photographs and verbatim testimony of children who had experienced abuse and neglect. I was involved in the physical removal of children from parents, child death inquiries and instructed counsel during contested custody and guardianship matters on behalf of the State in both the children's court and the family court jurisdictions. After a few years as a frontline child protection worker, I progressed to a Team Leader role where I managed other frontline child protection workers. Poorly at times in retrospect. Especially in relation to their wellbeing needs. I was 25 years old. I was in a new town, in a new office with new colleagues. I had moved there to take

DOI: 10.4324/9781003515371-1

up a locum position after my mother became unwell and died somewhat unexpectedly. I maintained a strict line between work and personal life, thinking this was a demonstration of my resilience. Evidence of my skills. Of course, in retrospect, that was naïve. I was overwhelmed on many fronts; however, I felt a sense of belonging and control in my ability to do the work. At the time, that seemed enough. That seemed like an achievement. This is the trap that many of us fall into.

Working with at-risk children and their families is often undertaken in an environment saturated in violence. Violence originating from the families of children involved in the system and at times from the system itself. Every day of those ten years working in statutory child protection, I experienced the threat of violence. I have often reflected on the fact that there is being yelled at and then there is being yelled at in the context of child protection work. As I write this, I can still feel the feeling of my heart stopping, the blood rushing to my head and all my senses feeling like they have jolted awake. It was routine for this to occur multiple times a day for years on end. I have experienced occupational traumatic stress symptomologies during my career that I found difficult to manage and that had the potential to derail my career. I have felt the deep shame and disappointment of not being able to carry on the job that I adored and saw myself doing long term because I could not resolve the occupational traumatic stress symptomology I was experiencing. I have experience seeking assistance for and overcoming these challenges and while I consider myself in recovery, recovery takes ongoing maintenance.

My doctoral research explored the previously unexplored experiences of First Nation's people who undertake child protection work and what their support needs might be 'working for the welfare'. One of the key learnings from my doctoral research was that although practitioners who identify as First Nations have some unique needs, there is something that binds all of us who work with at-risk children and their families together – the experience of occupational traumatic stress.

I guess one could question why people continue to do this work, given the complexities and challenges. For myself, I would say that working with at-risk children and their families is not black and white; it is grey. The grey is where the essence of our humanity lives, and it is exquisite. The TISS model is informed by my practice, personal and academic experience and summarises my commitment to supporting the practitioners who work in systems that support at-risk children and their families. You are important and you matter.

Throughout the book are vignettes highlighting the complexities of working with at-risk children and their families. For clarity, these vignettes include both verbatim accounts from practitioners and narratives that are a composition of my experience in both practice, research and higher education contexts. The vignettes have been included to demonstrate common challenges and dilemmas experienced by those working with at-risk children and their families, as they are extremely common and recurring.

## Introduction

Working with children at risk and their families is some of the most challenging work in the human, health and community services sector. Working with children at risk and their families requires a broad range of specialist skills and knowledge due to the complexity of these presentations. Since the Covid-19 pandemic, there has been a reported increase in the complexity of vulnerable families presenting to services due to the lack of affordable housing, stagnation of income support payments, shortages in the care workforce and the increase in the cost of essentials like food, transport, education and healthcare. These economic based factors have increased the demand on family support and related services as well as the number of children being notified to statutory child protection services across several jurisdictions.

As practitioners working with children at risk and their families, we are well versed in trauma and the challenges that people who have experienced significant trauma can encounter. When it comes to identifying trauma responses in ourselves as practitioners, this seems less straightforward. But why? Working with children at risk and their families is trauma-laden in nature, with the exposure to occupational traumatic stress an inevitability. Traditionally, organisations have struggled to provide their workforce with adequate support and supervision which is a key protective factor in supporting the wellbeing of practitioners. When practitioners begin to struggle with the symptomology of occupational traumatic stress in the workplace, too often they are labelled as not cut out for the role, not a team player, not resilient enough and/or problematic to the culture of the team. This can result in practitioners not being able to seek assistance when they start to experience symptoms consistent with occupational traumatic stress due to fear of being ostracised by their peers. It can also lead to practitioners internalising these struggles and attributing them to an innate deficiency within themselves rather than the symptoms being a result of an organisational culture that celebrates a lack of reaction to extreme situations as resilience rather than what it really is: a trauma response.

I developed the Trauma-Informed Support and Supervision (TISS) model to be a holistic, practitioner-centred framework that at its core normalises the experience of occupational traumatic stress. The TISS model acknowledges the complexity of the work, the organisational context that practitioners are working in and promotes the understanding that there are preventative strategies that can be put in place as well as ways to recover post symptoms presenting. The TISS model is a scaffolded model of support that centres practitioner wellbeing and development at the core. Supported practitioners are more likely to have the capacity to ensure that the care and protective needs of children at risk are assessed adequately and responded to effectively.

## Book structure

In this chapter, I will introduce a summarised version of the TISS model including the core elements of the framework. The evidence base that I relied on when developing the model will also be outlined. Following the introduction chapter, this book is divided into four parts. Part one explores the three central acknowledgements at the centre of the TISS model, namely, the experience of occupational trauma is an occupational inevitability; a practitioner's professional development and wellbeing support cannot be solely managed by their line supervisor or manager; and a practitioner's professional support needs will change over time. Part two outlines the trauma-informed principles, namely, safety; trustworthiness and transparency; peer support, collaboration and mutuality; empowerment, voice and choice; and cultural, historical and gender considerations, that underpin the TISS model. What trauma is and how it might occur in an occupational setting including typical symptomology, will also be discussed. Part three explores the four core pillars of the TISS model, namely the practitioner, the supervisor (and TISS team), the organisation and local contextualisation. Throughout parts one, two and three are reflective activities that invite practitioners to consider what their own needs might be, in their own personal and occupational context, through the framework of the TISS model. Working through these reflective activities will prepare practitioners to design and implement their own TISS plan in part four titled, creating and implementing a TISS model.

## What is child abuse and neglect?

In my first book about the TISS model, *Trauma-Informed Support and Supervision for Child Protection Professionals: a model for those working with children who have experienced trauma, abuse and neglect and their families*, I began the introduction chapter by defining what constitutes child abuse and neglect in an Anglo-Western context. I did that deliberately for two reasons. Firstly, because I wanted readers to have a uniform understanding of what constitutes child abuse and neglect, given that it was an introductory text that would be read by those who might be still studying through to those practitioners who are more established in their career. The second reason was to centre the kinds of traumas at-risk children and their families may have experienced, or continue to experience, which define the occupational context that practitioners are working in. In my own experience as a frontline practitioner working with at-risk children and their families, there exists a culture whereby the extreme nature of what practitioners are exposed to on a daily basis is minimised. Generic terms like 'offended against', 'sexually harmed', 'exposed to domestic violence', 'parental failure to protect', 'medically neglected', and 'excessive use of physical discipline' provide the opportunity for practitioners and organisations not to emotionally or intentionally engage with the extreme nature of the acts that constitute child abuse and neglect. It is my view that this may be the way practitioners protect their own wellbeing; however, more broadly, this practice can dilute the legitimacy of the experience and the following traumatic stress symptomologies.

I won't go into the same level of detail in this book; however, I will summarise what constitutes child abuse and neglect in the research and practice literature for those readers who have not read the first book. Child abuse and neglect can be characterised as a single event or a period of linked or unlinked events that occur in childhood, that is, between birth and 18 years of age. Harm from child abuse and neglect can be intrafamilial, meaning perpetrated by someone from within the family structure, or extra-familial, meaning someone outside of the family structure like peers, teachers, family friends, figures in faith-based settings and the like. While there is some variation in the literature about child abuse and neglect categories of harm, there is consensus on the four main harm types, namely, physical abuse, sexual abuse, emotional or psychological abuse and neglect.

Acts that may constitute physical harm to a child include, but are not limited to hitting, slapping, shaking, kicking, throwing, biting, burning, or poisoning. Physical harm that comes to a child from a parental figure's inaction, like a lack of supervision, can also constitute physical harm.

In relation to the sexual harm category, acts can include the penetration of a child in any way with another's body part or any other object, forcing a child to engage in sexual acts of any kind, exposing oneself to a child, exposing a child to sexual exploitation material that usually involves still or moving images of children being sexually abused, or engaging a child in prostitution. Actions that would constitute grooming of a child so that a perpetrator can eventually sexually abuse a child would also usually fall into the sexual harm category. Perpetrators can be adults or other peers, usually where there is a power imbalance like a gap in age or if the child in question has diminished capacity due to a disability or similar.

Emotional and psychological harm tend to be used interchangeably in the practice and research literature. What constitutes emotional or psychological harm varies in the literature and across jurisdictions. However, there is some consensus around the following acts that are consistent with this harm category like parental rejection, persistent threats of abandonment, hostility, scapegoating, sustained criticism and/or belittling. Other acts cited include educational or social isolation. Witnessing domestic violence is also sometimes included in this harm category.

The neglect category has some clear consensus in the literature about what core caregiver actions constitute neglect. These acts include withholding the basic necessities required for life like food, shelter, clothing, medical care and age-appropriate supervision, resulting in a significant threat, or risk of harm, to a child's health and wellbeing. Unlike the other harm categories, assessing whether a child has suffered neglect to a threshold requiring the State to intervene, is not always straightforward. An example might be a parent who has not provided adequate nutrition for their child to meet developmental milestones, however, they are living in an environment where access to food is restricted like a refugee settlement or an area impacted by a natural disaster. A practitioner may not assess this to be child abuse or neglect, as the parent had no ability to provide this due to their circumstances. Similarly, for families living in remote locations where access to health care is limited, assessments around harm may not always be clear, even though there would be occasions where lack of access to health care may be life-limiting for the child.

## Importance of broad practice contexts

In my first book about the TISS model, I went into detail about the diverse practice environments where professionals would find themselves working with at-risk children and their families. I included this section because there is a tendency in the research and practice literature to focus on child and family specific services when discussing the needs of practitioners working with this cohort. However, it must be acknowledged that almost all practitioners regardless of professional discipline working in social, health and community services will find themselves working with children at risk and their families. Health settings, education and training providers, housing and homelessness services, legal and justice services, emergency services, disability support and advocacy services and financial counselling settings, all provide service delivery in one way or another to vulnerable families including those families where child protection concerns that require further assessment might be present. Professionals working in these 'non-traditional' child protection settings are often overlooked in the research and practice literature and as such their supervision needs are not as well documented as their colleagues in statutory or community-based child protection services.

## What is trauma?

The concept of trauma is core to understanding and implementing the TISS model. I will summarise the key concepts of trauma, with further exploration in subsequent chapters. I define trauma as the psychological distress that remains with an individual after exposure to traumatic occurrences. The remnants of these events can also remain in our bodies as physical symptomology. These remnants may present in a myriad of ways and may look different to what others expect a trauma response to look like – especially in the context of the workplace. Occupational trauma exposure occurs in the context of a person's employment. The symptomology of occupational traumatic stress presents similarly to the experience of trauma in a non-occupational setting (Graham, 2012; Rubino et al., 2009). Occupational traumatic stress symptomology and how it presents in the workplace are explored extensively in the next chapter.

While community and intergenerational trauma are not the focus of this book, it is worth noting that communities and generations who have experienced significant traumatic events like war, colonisation and occupation can have a collective experience of trauma which can be passed down to generations who themselves did not directly experience the trauma.

In the research literature, trauma is described as a normal physiological response to a single event or series of events that are extreme or threatening in nature (Haskell & Randall, 2009). The Substance Abuse and Mental Health Services Administration (SAMHSA) provides the following definition of trauma, namely:

> Individual trauma results from an event, series of events or set of circumstances that is experienced by an individual as physically or emotionally harmful or life threatening and that has lasting adverse effects on the individual's functioning and mental, physical, social, emotional or spiritual wellbeing.
>
> (SAMHSA, 2014, p. 7)

The International Society for Traumatic Stress Studies (ISTSS) adds that traumatic events that lead a person to feel overwhelmed or unable to cope with the resulting negative emotions can be the events that lead to ongoing experiences of traumatic stress symptomology. ISTSS also state that events which are interpersonal or intentional in nature, including childhood abuse and neglect, tend to be responsible for a greater experience of adverse psychological outcomes (ISTSS, 2022).

## What is supervision?

The definition of supervision I relied on in my first book about the TISS model is the same definition I have relied on in this book which comes from Davys and Beddoe (2010), who cite that professional supervision is:

> a forum for reflection and learning . . . an interactive dialogue between at least two people, one of whom is a supervisor. This dialogue shapes a process of review, reflection, critique and replenishment for professional practitioners. Supervision is a professional activity in which practitioners are engaged throughout the duration of their careers regardless of experience or qualification. The participants are accountable to professional standards and defined competencies and to organisational policy and procedures.
>
> (p. 21)

In the research and practice literature, there is consensus on the three key elements that should be present in any professional supervision practice. These three elements are administrative, educational and supportive (Beddoe & Davys, 2016; Berger & Quiros, 2016; Kadushin and Harkness, 2014; Tsui, 2005). In addition to the three traditional elements, a fourth element, mediation, was introduced into the research literature by Rankine (2019). The fourth element of mediation, in my view, should be a core inclusion in supervision practice. I will now briefly summarise these four elements and will discuss them more in depth in the following chapters in the context of the TISS model.

The administration element of supervision focuses on needs that are organisationally driven. This might include things like progress on key deliverables, workload management, matters pertaining to contractual compliance or HR-related matters like timesheets, leave management or completion of mandatory training like fire safety procedures, management, and storage of chemicals. While all of these things are important and necessary, there is consistent criticism in the research literature that supervision provided to practitioners by their line managers is too focused on administrative tasks, neglecting the wellbeing and development needs of staff (Hunt et al., 2016; Goddard & Hunt, 2011; Oates, 2019).

The educational element of supervision practice focuses on the professional development of the practitioner including canvassing formal and informal opportunities for professional growth. Brittain (2009) argues that the core purpose of the educational element in supervision is to furnish the practitioner with the skills, knowledge, experiences, and attitudes required to successfully undertake their duties. Formal opportunities for the learning and integration of knowledge into practice may be the request for funds for a practitioner to attend specialist training or to subscribe to a professional peer-reviewed journal as a strategy to keep practitioner knowledge current. Informal opportunities may include engaging in live supervision where a practitioner accompanies a more experienced practitioner, possibly the line supervisor, on home visits or to meetings where they can observe the application of professional knowledge into practice with clients and other stakeholders. A critically reflective session after such an opportunity presents a real and tangible space for a practitioner to solidify their knowledge base and increase their professional capacity to undertake their role successfully.

The supportive element of supervision relates to practitioner wellbeing matters including how a practitioner might be managing the stress of their current workload, strategies to mediate feelings of overwhelm and other elements such as if a practitioner is achieving a work/life balance. The support element of supervision is cited in the research literature as a key strategy in assisting practitioners to manage the impact of occupational traumatic stress and related stressors (Hunt et al., 2016; Kadushin & Harkness, 2014). Additionally, the support element of supervision is linked to increased levels of job satisfaction. The relationship between job satisfaction and practitioner wellbeing will be explored further in subsequent chapters; however, to summarise, job satisfaction is cited in the research literature as leading to increased motivation, good morale within teams and a sustained commitment to the organisation a practitioner works for, leading to better rates of staff retention (Kantabutra & Ketprapakorn, 2021).

Deviating from the traditional three pillars of supervision is Morrison's (2001) inclusion of mediation as a fourth pillar. Morrison (2001) describes the mediation element of supervision to support a balance between practice knowledge and development including wellbeing support as well as the exploration of tensions that exist between the practitioner and the organisation. This element speaks to the ongoing negotiation in supervision between the needs and agenda of the practitioner and the needs and agenda of the organisation. Often, these needs are in opposition to each other, creating a potential source of conflict within the supervision process.

## What is the TISS model?

The TISS model is a scaffolded support and supervision framework designed to support the wellbeing and professional development needs of professionals working with at-risk children and their families, regardless of their professional or discipline-specific background. The TISS framework is underpinned by three central acknowledgements, namely, the experience of occupational trauma is an occupational inevitability; a practitioner's professional development and wellbeing support cannot be solely managed by their line supervisor or manager; and a practitioner's professional support needs will change over time; the six trauma-informed principles, namely, safety; trustworthiness and transparency; peer support, collaboration and mutuality; empowerment, voice and choice; and cultural, historical and gender considerations; and the four core pillars, namely, the practitioner, the supervisor (and TISS team), the organisation and local contextualisation. The purpose of the framework is to guide professionals to develop their own TISS plan. A TISS team is comprised of people, including the practitioner, who will work towards supporting the wellbeing and professional development of the individual practitioner. The TISS plan is the plan that the TISS team will use to achieve this.

I will now briefly summarise these key elements that form the TISS model as well as the TISS plan and TISS team concepts, including the evidence base that informs them, in more depth over the coming chapters.

## Central acknowledgements

The TISS framework is built on three central acknowledgements, that is, acknowledgements that are accepted as truth. The first central acknowledgement is that the experience of occupational traumatic stress is an occupational inevitability. The second central acknowledgement is that a practitioner's professional development and wellbeing support cannot be solely managed by their line supervisor. The final central acknowledgement is that a practitioner's professional support needs will change over time. I will summarise these three central acknowledgements in this chapter and then explore them more deeply in the coming chapters.

The **first acknowledgement**, the experience of occupational traumatic stress is an occupational inevitability, is the first and in many ways the core of the TISS model. As previously mentioned, working with at-risk children and their families is complex and requires practitioners to have broad knowledge and skills. It also requires that practitioners work in often volatile situations, with people who are surviving in chaos and crisis, without always having the resources to support them. Practitioners require specialist supervision and support that nurtures

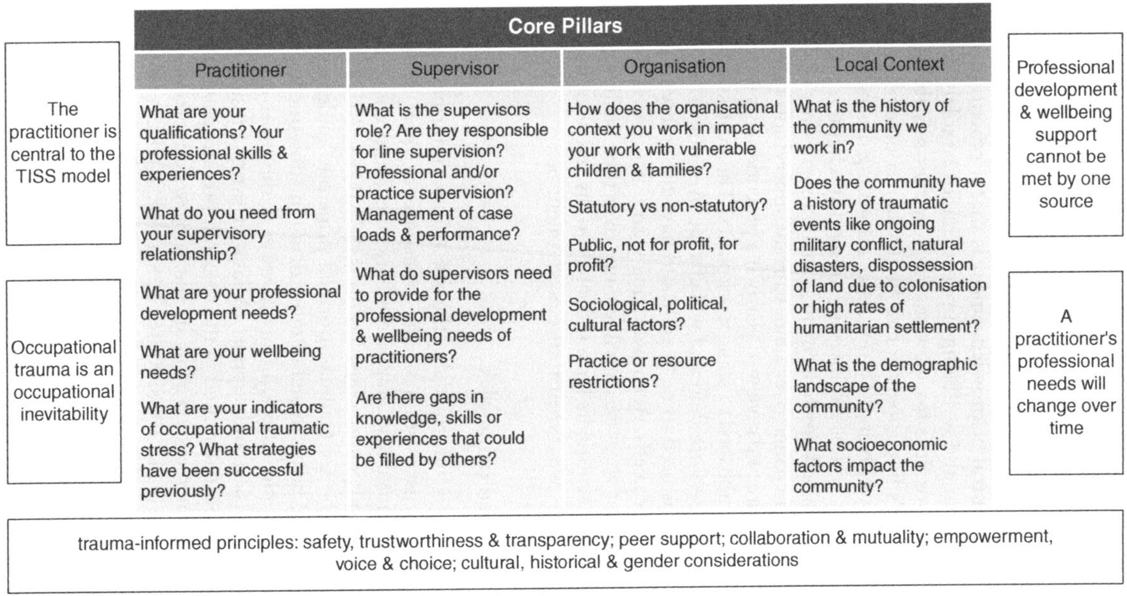


*Figure 0.1* TISS Framework.

them as practitioners in the workplace but also as people working in a trauma-laden environment. No one works in this field and is not in some way impacted by what they hear, see and experience. The practitioner experience of occupational traumatic stress is inevitable and therefore requires an organisational response that normalises this actuality that is practitioner-centred and has a preventative and post-exposure focus – the TISS model provides the framework for such a response.

The **second central acknowledgement** is that a practitioner's professional development and wellbeing support cannot be solely managed by their line supervisor. It is my view that it is neither possible nor ethical for a practitioner's line supervisor to be the sole source of professional development and wellbeing. The evidence informing the inclusion of this acknowledgement will be explored in subsequent chapters.

The **final central acknowledgement** is that a practitioner's professional support needs will change over time. Current supervision processes tend to be static in nature and reviewed yearly if a practitioner is lucky or never again after it is established in some workplaces. The professional support needs of practitioners are fluid and will change over time for a number of reasons. TISS plans need to be flexible and have the ability to be responsive to practitioner needs. Acknowledging with practitioners that there is an expectation that their needs will change over time facilitates an environment where practitioners have the safety to discuss what their current needs are as well as what their future needs might be.

## Trauma-informed principles

The TISS model is informed by the six trauma-informed principles, namely, safety; trustworthiness and transparency; peer support, collaboration and mutuality; empowerment, voice, and choice; and cultural, historical and gender considerations (SAMHSA, 2014). I will now summarise how the six trauma-informed principles underpin the TISS model. All six will be discussed in more detail in subsequent chapters.

The first principle, **safety**, in many ways is the most critical in the context of supervision and support. A lack of safety in the supervisory relationship is repeatedly cited in the research literature as a barrier for effective practitioner engagement in the supervision process (Kruzich et al., 2014; Little et al., 2018; Radey & Stanley, 2018). A lack of safety in supervision can also inform a practitioner's decision not to disclose matters that might be impacting their wellbeing in the workplace including symptoms of occupational traumatic stress (Beddoe et al., 2014; McFadden, 2020; Regehr, 2018; Oates, 2019).

The second principle, **trustworthiness and transparency**, in the context of the TISS model, relates to transparency in the supervisory relationship including what the purpose of supervision is and what the sessions might be used for. A number of participants in my own research indicated that at times they were suspicious about what supervision was and believed that the sessions were used by their line supervisors as a strategy to performance manage them out of their positions (Oates, 2019). The building and maintenance of trust in the supervisory relationship is critical and has been identified in the research literature as a key factor in a practitioner's ability to move through traumatic occupational experiences.

The third principle, **peer support**, in the context of the TISS model refers to the support a practitioner receives from their peers in either a formal or informal capacity. Usually, peer support comes from those who are colleagues, not involved in the practitioner's line supervision. In my own research, several participants felt a greater sense of safety to share exactly what they have been experiencing with someone (peer or supervisor) who had also worked with at-risk children and their families, feeling that unless you have done this kind of work, you can never fully understand what it is like and therefore the impacts. There is also a feeling that practitioners who undertake work with children who have experienced abuse and neglect don't want to share all the details with someone who hasn't done that work because they don't want to traumatise them. This intrinsic sense of responsibility to others is admirable; however, it can block a practitioner's ability to fully engage with supports. I explore this phenomenon in subsequent chapters.

The fourth principle, **collaboration and mutuality**, in the context of the TISS model, relates to the partnership element of supervision. The TISS model recognises the practitioner as an equal member within their own TISS team with the ability to define goals and design the steps to achieve those goals. Power constructs and how they may impede a practitioner's ability to fully participate in their own TISS plan need to be kept on the TISS team's agenda and reviewed regularly.

The fifth principle, **empowerment, voice and choice**, relates to a practitioner's ability to be able to name what supports, including the type of supervision, they require to be able to effectively undertake their role. This may seem on the surface to be straightforward; however, practitioners are inducted into this vocation in a myriad of ways. Some of those ways may include hierarchical or toxic organisational cultures where supervision arrangements may have not been prioritised, been predominantly task-focused or where the supervisor was positioned as the expert and the practitioner as a passive receiver of supervision. A practitioner may never have had a 'good' supervision experience and therefore may not be able to name what it is that they need or what a responsive practitioner-centred arrangement might look like for them. Examples may have to be provided in some instances. Further, some practitioners may need to be supported to add or subtract supports as individual circumstances change.

The final principle, **cultural, historical, and gender considerations**, in the context of the TISS model, refers to sources of support that may assist a practitioner in feeling safest to fully engage with supervision. Examples could include a female-identifying practitioner who may wish to receive support from another female-identifying professional. This may be to reduce interruption from patriarchal oppression (real or perceived) and may create an opportunity for a practitioner to engage more fully with supports. Another example could be a practitioner's desire to engage in supports with another practitioner of the same cultural or language background, again to remove barriers to participation and increase the effectiveness of supports. The TISS model is a practitioner-centred model and therefore it is important never to assume what a practitioner may need. It is critical to always ask and to keep checking in as a practitioner's needs may change over time.

## Four core pillars

There are four core pillars to the TISS model. These pillars are the practitioner, the supervisor (and TISS team), the organisation, and local contextualisation. Working through these core pillars will form the basis of a practitioner's TISS plan. As with the other core elements, I will introduce and summarise the individual pillars in this chapter and explore them in more depth in the coming chapters.

**The practitioner pillar**: Practitioners are at the centre of the TISS model. There would be no work with at-risk children and their families without them. Practitioners are central to ensuring the care and protection needs of at-risk children are assessed and appropriately responded to. Elements to consider within this pillar are what the practitioner's motivation to undertake this work might be, where their internal pressure points might be, strategies a practitioner may have used in the past to manage occupational traumatic stress, a thorough exploration of what the practitioners existing skills, knowledge and qualifications are as well as what a practitioner's professional interests and aspirations might be.

**The supervisor (and TISS team) pillar**: The supervisor pillar relates to the line supervisor within the TISS team. This is usually the person supervising a practitioner's work within their organisation. This pillar also relates to members of the TISS team which could include a paid external provider of external supervision or a senior practitioner within the practitioner's organisation, who does not have line supervision responsibilities as examples. Similar to the practitioner pillar, line managers, supervisors, and others involved in a practitioner's TISS team will also have a myriad of motivations for undertaking the role that they do in the context of working with at-risk children and their families. As already outlined, transparency is a core principle informing the TISS model. Therefore, those participating in the model will need to thoroughly reflect on how much information about themselves they are willing to contribute. It is also important to have a frank and mature conversation about what a practitioner needs from their line supervisor and then to plan for the gaps to be filled by an alternative method of support.

**The organisation pillar**: The organisation pillar relates to the organisation that a practitioner works for. It can also, in some circumstances, relate to the organisation, usually a government department, that funds the organisation or programme a practitioner works in. The inclusion of the examination of the organisational environment in which a practitioner works in a supervision context is unique to the TISS model. It is clear in the research literature, which will be discussed in detail in the coming chapters, that many organisations struggle to provide effective supervision to their workforce for a myriad of reasons. Some of those reasons include staff shortages, inability for an organisation to finance external supervision, organisational cultures that don't value or prioritise supervision, crisis-driven organisational environments where planning for such sessions can be difficult, and misalignment of professional backgrounds between practitioners and those supervising them. Acknowledging these shortcomings organisationally with the practitioner in the context of supervision will normalise these deficits and provide the practitioner with an opportunity to identify other sources of support that more adequately meet their individual needs. This is consistent with the second central acknowledgement of the TISS model, namely, that a practitioner's professional development and wellbeing support cannot be solely managed by their line supervisor.

**The local contextualisation pillar**: The local contextualisation pillar relates to the place-based considerations that exist within the physical community that a practitioner is working in. Similar to the organisation pillar, the inclusion of the examination of the local community in which a practitioner works is unique to the TISS model. The size of the community, the socio/economic/political make-up of the community, access to universal services like health, housing and education, the settlement history, natural disaster or conflict history, and the dominant cultural background of the community will all impact practitioners working in those communities. Examining the benefits and challenges of living in the community a practitioner is working in, especially in the context of working with at-risk children and their families, is an important element of the TISS model. As an example, the smaller the community is that a practitioner might work in, the more likely it will be that they will come into contact with children and families they have worked with outside of their work hours. Examples could include having children attend the same school, attending the same place of worship, or participating in the same sporting or social group. There may be limited places to shop for essentials like groceries, medication, or fuel. The smaller the community, the more visible a practitioner becomes which can lead to increased feelings of pressure and/or isolation. Understanding these elements and being able to analyse community issues from this framework is a strategy that will facilitate a practitioner's ability to externalise some of the occupational traumatic stress they may experience as a result of working with at-risk children and their families.

## The TISS plan

Tying it all together, the TISS plan is the map forward in supporting the professional development and wellbeing needs of the practitioner. The TISS plan will outline all the members of the TISS team, as well as their roles and responsibilities. As mentioned earlier, the TISS plan is informed by the three central acknowledgements, the six trauma-informed principles, and the four core pillars. The TISS model seeks to identify and plan for these research-informed factors so that practitioners have the best opportunity to receive support and supervision that meets both their professional development and wellbeing needs. The coming chapters include a number of reflective activities that practitioners can engage with to inform the development and implementation of their own TISS plan.

## Chapter summary

In this chapter, the TISS model was introduced. Key elements that form that model were summarised including the three central acknowledgements, namely, the experience of occupational trauma is an occupational inevitability; a practitioner's professional development and wellbeing support cannot be solely managed by their line supervisor or manager; and a practitioner's professional support needs will change over time; the six trauma-informed principles, namely, safety; trustworthiness and transparency; peer support, collaboration and mutuality; empowerment, voice and choice; and cultural, historical and gender considerations, and the four core pillars, namely, the practitioner, the supervisor (and TISS team), the organisation, and local contextualisation. Trauma as a concept was summarised including occupational traumatic trauma exposure. Supervision was also summarised to give a shared understanding through subsequent chapters. In the following chapters, the key elements of the TISS model introduced in this chapter will be more thoroughly explored. Opportunities will also be presented by way of reflective activities to assist practitioners in thinking about the kinds of things they would include in their own TISS plans.

## References


Beddoe, L., & Davys, A. (2016). *Challenges in professional supervision: Current themes and models for practice*. London: Jessica Kingsley Publishers.

Beddoe, L., Davys, A., & Adamson, C. (2014). "Never trust anybody who says 'I don't need supervision'": Practitioners beliefs about social worker resilience. *Practice (Birmingham, England)*, *26*(2), 113–130. https://doi.org/10.1080/09503153.2014.896888

Berger, R., & Quiros, L. (2016). Best practices for training trauma-informed practitioners: Supervisors' voice. *Traumatology*, *22*(2), 145–154. https://doi.org/10.1037/trm0000076

Brittain, C. (2009). Models of social work supervision. In C. Potter & C. Brittain (Eds.), *Child welfare supervision: A practical guide for supervisors, managers and administrators* (pp. 23–43). New York: Oxford University Press.

Davys, A., & Beddoe, L. (2010). *Best practice in professional supervision: A guide for the helping professions*. London, England: Jessica Kingsley.

Goddard, C., & Hunt, S. (2011). The complexities of caring for child protection workers: The contexts of practice and supervision. *Journal of Social Work Practice*, *25*(4), 413–432. https://doi.org/0.1080/02650533.2011.626644

Graham, J. (2012). Cognitive behavioural therapy for occupational trauma: A systematic literature review exploring the effects of occupational trauma and the existing CBT support pathways and interventions for staff working within mental healthcare including allied professions. *Cognitive Behaviour Therapist*, *5*(1), 24–45. https://doi.org/10.1017/S1754470X12000025

Haskell, L., & Randall, M. (2009). Disrupted attachments: A social context complex trauma framework and the lives of aboriginal peoples in Canada. *Journal of Aboriginal Health*, *5*(3), 48.

Hunt, S., Goddard, C., Cooper, J., Littlechild, B., & Wild, J. (2016). "If I feel like this, how does the child feel?" Child protection workers, supervision, management and organisational responses to parental violence. *Journal of Social Work Practice*, *30*(1), 5–24. https://doi.org/10.1080/02650533.2015.1073145

International Society for Traumatic Stress Studies. (2022, January 5). *Trauma basics*. https://istss.org/public-resources/trauma-basics

Kadushin, A., & Harkness, D. (2014). *Supervision in social work* (5th ed.). Columbia University Press.

Kantabutra, S., & Ketprapakorn, N. (2021). Toward an organizational theory of resilience: An interim struggle. *Sustainability*, *13*(23). https://doi.org/10.3390/su132313137

Kruzich, J., Mienko, J., & Courtney, M. (2014). Individual and work group influences on turnover intention among public child welfare workers: The effects of work group psychological safety. *Children and Youth Services Review*, *42*, 20–27. https://doi.org/10.1016/j.childyouth.2014.03.005

Little, M., Baker, T., & Jinks, A. (2018). A qualitative evaluation of community nurses' experiences of child safeguarding supervision. *Child Abuse Review*, *27*(2), 150–157. http://dx.doi.org/10.1002/car.2493

McFadden, P. (2020). Two sides of one coin? Relationships build resilience or contribute to burnout in child protection social work: Shared perspectives from leavers and stayers in Northern Ireland. *International Social Work*, *63*(2), 164–176. https://doi.org/10.1177/0020872818788393

Morrison, T. (2001). *Staff supervision in social care: Making a real difference for staff and service users*. Brighton: Pavilion.

Oates, F. (2019). You are not allowed to tell: Organisational culture as a barrier for child protection workers seeking assistance for traumatic stress symptomology. *Children Australia*, *44*(2), 84–90. https://doi.org/10.1017/cha.2019.12

Radey, M., & Stanley, L. (2018). "Hands on" versus "empty": Supervision experiences of frontline child welfare workers. *Children and Youth Services Review*, *91*, 128–136. https://doi.org/10.1016/j.childyouth.2018.05.037

Rankine, M. (2019). The internal/external debate: The tensions within social work supervision. *Aotearoa New Zealand Social Work*, *31*(3), 32–45. https://doi.org/10.11157/anzswj-vol31iss3id646

Regehr, C. (2018). *Stress, trauma, and decision-making for social workers*. New York: Columbia University Press.

Rubino, C., Luksyte, A., Perry, S., & Volpone, S. (2009). How do stressors lead to burnout? The mediating role of motivation. *Journal of Occupational Health Psychology*, *14*(3), 289–304. https://doi.org/10.1037/a0015284

Substance Abuse and Mental Health Services Administration. (2014). *SAMHSA's concept of trauma and guidance for a trauma informed approach*. Rockville, MD: Substance Abuse and Mental Health Services Administration.

Tsui, M. (2005). *Social work supervision: Contexts and concepts*. SAGE Publications.

# Part one Central acknowledgements that inform the TISS model

## Introduction

The TISS model is a scaffolded supervision model underpinned by three central acknowledgements, the six recognised trauma-informed principles, and four core pillars. This chapter explores the three central acknowledgements in depth, namely, the experience of occupational trauma is an occupational inevitability; a practitioner's professional development and wellbeing support cannot be solely managed by their line supervisor or manager; and a practitioner's professional support needs will change over time. How the central acknowledgements can inform a practitioner's TISS plan will also be explored. Opportunities will be provided to engage in reflective activities which are woven throughout the chapter. These activities guide practitioners to think about how the central acknowledgements resonate with them either professionally, personally, or both in preparation for the completion of their own TISS plan within their own occupational context.

## The experience of occupational trauma is an occupational inevitability

Working with at-risk children and their families is a difficult and challenging vocation. The nature of the work exposes practitioners to occupational trauma and violence. The experience of occupational traumatic stress is an occupational inevitability. The TISS model acknowledges this reality without qualification. Acknowledging that occupational trauma exposure is an inevitability doesn't mean that practitioners shouldn't be supported through their occupational traumatic stress symptomology. They should be supportedvin a way that validates their experience and doesn't erode their ability to work in the field.

In the introduction chapter of this book, I outlined the importance of acknowledging the primary trauma that practitioners who work with at-risk children and their families are routinely exposed to.

DOI: 10.4324/9781003515371-2

Primary trauma exposure is often overlooked in the research literature which in my view leads to a minimisation of these events and the subsequent occupational traumatic stress symptomology that can be experienced by practitioners as a result. In addition, a lack of attention to this area has led to a dearth of research about how best to support practitioners to work through experiences of occupational traumatic stress that are difficult to resolve, especially in an organisational context. By highlighting primary trauma exposure, I am in no way minimising the very real impacts of vicarious and secondary trauma; I am simply highlighting the need for a focus on an existing gap that is highly relevant to practitioners who work in the trauma-laden environment that is child protection.

The research literature outlines a number of impacts on practitioners who experience occupational traumatic stress symptomology. These include a decrease in job satisfaction and performance (Hunt et al., 2016; Whinghter et al., 2008), poor self-esteem and self-image (Oates, 2019; Regehr, 2018), inability to connect with relationships personal and professional (Oates, 2019), as well as symptomology consistent with anxiety and depression including formation of maladaptive coping strategies like an increase in alcohol and other substance use (Hunt et al., 2016; Graham, 2012; Oates, 2019; Regehr, 2018).

The first central acknowledgement in many ways was the genesis of the TISS model. As previously mentioned, I myself have experienced occupational traumatic stress symptomologies that I found difficult to manage as a result of being exposed to a myriad of primary trauma experiences while working with at-risk children and their families. During that time, I found it extremely difficult to manage the internal dialogue that I in some way was responsible for these symptoms as it appeared no one else around me was experiencing the same thing. I loved my job and a large part of my identify was rooted in my ability to work in that field and to successfully navigate the challenges and complexities. I found comfort, connection and understanding with others who worked in the same field. Losing that sense of belonging and connection when I left my role was in many ways more traumatising than the events that caused the symptomology and the symptomology itself.

While undertaking my doctoral research, many of the participants I interviewed described an almost identical experience of feeling that they were the only ones being impacted by occupational stress symptomology, making them deficient in the skills required to do their job. Many participants described their inner dialogue being mirrored back to them by their colleagues and their organisation. Research participants, as well as supervisees I have worked with, talked about the gatekeeping they experienced in the workplace from other staff if they talked about distressing incidents or if they started to experience symptoms of occupational traumatic stress. Some experiences are listed below:

> *They would say – Do you think that's really something you should be talking about around the office? Aren't you worried that you'll lose your job?*
>
> – Alice

> *I went to a home with a female police officer to interview a father about the injuries his teenaged daughter said he caused. He was so aggressive that the police officer told him to come to the police station to continue the interview. We were in a small interview room with him and it all happened so quickly – he got up and blocked the doorway so we couldn't get out. He was explosively angry, threatening us – I was terrified about what would happen next and I just froze – that had never happened to me before. It ended with him storming out – I was still frozen and numb so I just sat there in the interview room. After it all was over, I drove back to the office and told my team leader – she said incidents like that were part of the job and I should grow a spine*
>
> – Audrey

> *I went and saw the manager about it, and she said yeah, well maybe child safety work isn't for you, maybe you could work in projects or do a different job somewhere else*
>
> – Rosalyn

> *I'm being told maybe you're not suited to your role in [statutory child protection]. I've been here [number] years, but okay, whatever*
>
> – Sarah

While many acknowledged the exposure to the horrors of child abuse, injustice and oppression to be difficult, many described the trauma of being expelled from the work group, feeling dislocated from their profession and vocation, to be the central trauma they were unable to resolve:

> *I went on stress leave to clear my head. I had not been sleeping for months and was completely overwhelmed to the point where I was not functioning at home – I was letting my kids down, not connecting with my partner. I decided I needed to leave. I emailed my resignation. A few weeks later a 'sorry you are leaving' card arrived in the mail. Other than that, I never heard from my colleagues in that office again. I had worked there for 4 years. It was devastating*
>
> – Ingrid

> *The first time I had to go out to my old office for a meeting, I had a panic attack. Yeah, it was really, really difficult. Yeah, it's just whenever I talk about it, like I am now, I get that thumping feeling in my gut*
>
> – Matilda

Since the publication of my first book about the TISS model, *Trauma-Informed Support and Supervision for Child Protection Professionals: a model for those working with children who have experienced trauma, abuse and neglect and their families*, I have had several practitioners reach out to share their experiences which are identical to my own and to those practitioners above. It is my firm view that the continued discarding of practitioners who experience occupational traumatic stress symptomology because systems are ill-prepared to manage these presentations, contributes to the high turnover of staff, adding additional risk to already vulnerable children and families.

Imagine if there was a genuine organisational acknowledgement that the experience of occupational trauma and related symptomologies was an occupational inevitability? The change in the way the symptoms are experienced and viewed organisationally would completely change, leading more practitioners to successfully manage their symptoms and minimise their impact on their professional and personal lives. It would also enable organisations to retain experienced practitioners within the sector workforce which can only lead to better outcomes for at-risk children and their families.

## Reflective activity

- Reflect on your own experiences, do you have an internal dialogue that connects the experience of occupational traumatic stress and not being skilled enough to work with at-risk children and their families?
- If yes, reflect on where you think this thought process came from? What can be done to counteract this narrative?

Notes:

______________________________________________

______________________________________________

______________________________________________

______________________________________________

______________________________________________

______________________________________________

## A practitioner's professional development and wellbeing support cannot be solely managed by their line supervisor or manager

The second central acknowledgement informing the TISS model is that a practitioner's professional development and wellbeing support cannot be solely managed by their line supervisor or manager. I acknowledge that this is a deviation from many traditional supervision models; however, the research literature tells us organisations that deliver services to at-risk children and their families struggle to provide effective support and supervision to their workforce (Beddoe & Davys, 2016; Hunt et al., 2016; Oates, 2019). Several reasons for this are cited in the literature including resourcing, organisational culture and practitioner perception (Beddoe & Davys, 2016; Hunt et al., 2016; McCrae et al., 2015; Oates, 2019).

The quality of internal supervision, that is, supervision provided by a practitioner's line supervisor, is also criticised in the research literature, especially in statutory contexts. Studies by Manthorpe et al. (2015); Wilkins et al. (2017); and Goddard and Hunt (2011) all found that supervision available to practitioners working with at-risk children and their families tended to be heavily weighted towards compliance, driven by organisational agendas and lacked a clear focus on reflective practice and practitioner wellbeing. Below are three examples shared by practitioners about the quality of supervision they experienced and the impact it can have when there is not a strong focus on practitioner wellbeing:

> *I think it's good to have supervision with your [line supervisor]. I think that's required, I think that's needed. I think cases need to be discussed. But on the other hand, [practitioners] need to have that emotional debriefing about how it's impacting on them along the way . . . supervision [at statutory agency] was more about getting the job done, paperwork-based type thing, compared to worrying about how I felt or what I was going through at the time. It was very bang, bang, bang, get the job done, bang, bang, bang, get the paperwork done. 'You should have this, this and this done by now. Why haven't you?*
>
> – Rosalyn

> *It certainly wasn't about my wellbeing and it was generally me organising it. But definitely not about me, that's why I burnt out, because I had no support*
>
> – Matilda

> *I would always get so anxious before supervision. My supervisor would fire questions at me about where cases were up to – the workload was so big I never could catch up so I was always getting told to do better. My supervisor never really asked how I was coping so I didn't mention it, but I was really drowning*
>
> – Kaye

The supervisory relationship is a protective factor identified in a practitioner's ability to successfully navigate occupational traumatic stress symptomology (Davys & Beddoe, 2010; Pack, 2015). The creation and maintenance of trust and safety within the supervisory relationship was explored in the previous chapter as a critical element needed.

There is some consensus in the research literature about the attributes possessed by successful supervisors as defined by those receiving supervision. These characteristics included availability, consistency and predictability (Berger & Quiros, 2016; McPherson et al., 2016; Radey & Stanley, 2018), acknowledgement of own limitations and humility (Berger & Quiros, 2016); fostering a learning and professional development culture (Berger & Quiros, 2016; Little et al., 2018); valued staff (McPherson et al., 2016); experienced and knowledgeable (Kouzes & Posner, 2016; Rankine, 2019), empathetic, self-regulating and encouraging of self-care (Abassary & Goodrich, 2014; McPherson et al., 2016; Radey & Stanley, 2018). Below is an example of how a practitioner's wellbeing can be negatively impacted in an occupational context when trust and safety in the supervisory relationship have not been established:

> *I worked in a program supporting families where the caregiver had a mental health condition. I was drawn to the role because my mother had a mental health condition and I understand what is like for children growing up in that environment, especially the judgement from service providers and the fear of being reported to child welfare authorities. My supervisor knew everything about the legislation, case management, referral pathways etc. However, I just didn't feel I could share my background with them. I didn't feel safe. I was worried about where that information might end up or that she might think I couldn't do the job because of my background. I felt they wouldn't understand so I remained silent about it.*
>
> – Joella

Not all line supervisory relationships will have the capacity for safety and trust to be built for several reasons. In the case of Joella* above, it is clear that an external supervisor would be best placed to provide the kind of support and supervision that would have assisted her. Given the broad knowledge and skill base practitioners require to work with at-risk children and families and the diverse needs of the workforce, it is not possible for one line supervisor to provide the spectrum of support and supervision arrangements required to effectively meet the needs of practitioners. Additionally, given the nature of occupational traumatic stress and how symptomology can present, there are practical but also ethical considerations that need to be taken into account if the only source of wellbeing support available to practitioners is via their line supervisor or manager.

Considering the evidence that positive supervisory relationships correlate with practitioner wellbeing, increased levels of job satisfaction and increased practitioner retention, and the consistent criticism that organisations struggle to provide effective supervision, perhaps it is time to critically reflect on the role of the line supervisor. Should line supervisors and managers be the primary source of support and supervision for practitioners working with at-risk children and their families? Should they be primarily responsible for the induction and ongoing mentoring of new practitioners, particularly given their workloads? Is it ethical for line supervisors and managers to have the dual role of practitioner performance management and the central point for practitioners to access support for wellbeing matters? Would diffusing these critical roles to other modes of support be more beneficial for the practitioner? For the line supervisor or manager?

Given the struggles organisations experience in consistently providing high-quality and effective supervision, it is my view that it is time to rethink the role of the line supervisor in the support and supervision arrangements of practitioners working with at-risk children and their families. This is why this central acknowledgement has been included in the TISS model.

## Reflective activity

- Thinking about your line supervisor or manager, write down what you are comfortable disclosing to them. What are you not comfortable disclosing to them within supervision?
- Thinking of the things that you are not comfortable disclosing in supervision, what other sources of support could you rely on to meet these needs?

Notes:

## A practitioner's professional support needs will change over time

The third central acknowledgement informing the TISS model is that a practitioner's professional support needs will change over time. This central acknowledgement has been included as it relates to job satisfaction. In the previous chapter, I outlined that job satisfaction was frequently cited in the literature as being a critical element that contributes to practitioners remaining in their roles working with at-risk children and their families (Beddoe et al., 2014; Berger & Quiros, 2016; Hunt et al., 2016; Regehr, 2018). A practitioner's support and professional development needs are fluid and will ebb and flow over time as they become more experienced in their roles. Practitioner's feeling stagnant in their professional development may feel compelled to look elsewhere if they are not supported in their roles to grow and to see additional opportunities:

> *I had been in my family support role for a couple of years. I had a wonderful supervisor. However long term I wanted to transition more into expressive therapies and counselling with children. My supervisor at the time had no experience in this area. I mentioned it to them multiple times in supervision, but they never encouraged me to pursue my interest in the area. It made me feel that supervision wasn't the place to discuss it so I stopped.*
>
> – Kristen

> *I was really keen to do more leadership type roles within my organisation. I had been working in human services for 12 years and felt a bit uninspired. I really craved something new, but I didn't want to leave my organisation. I had always had good*

> *supervisors however just doing the same case work wasn't enough anymore. I felt stuck.*
>
> – Andy

Reviews need to be an ingrained part of the process to capture what a practitioner's current needs are so that they can be catered for. Aspirational needs also need to be identified and catered for. Additionally, reviews be needed in response to unplanned changes in circumstances like after a critical incident or a change in life circumstances as examples.

### Reflective activity

- What gives you the feeling of job satisfaction?
- What part of your current role makes you 'feel stuck' like Andy*?
- What are your career progression goals?
- Consider what your support and professional development needs might look like in 1, 3 and 5 years' time to help you achieve those career goals.

Notes:

________________________________________
________________________________________
________________________________________
________________________________________
________________________________________

## Chapter summary

In this chapter, I have explored the three central acknowledgements that inform the TISS model, namely, the experience of occupational trauma is an occupational inevitability; a practitioner's professional development and wellbeing support cannot be solely managed by their line supervisor or manager; and a practitioner's professional support needs will change over time. Reflective activities were also woven throughout the chapter to assist practitioners with considering what they would like to include in their own TISS plans. It is important when preparing one's own TISS plan to have these central acknowledgements in mind, as they are the basis of the TISS model.

## References

Abassary, C., & Goodrich, K. M. (2014). Attending to crisis-based supervision for counselors: The CARE model of crisis-based supervision. *The Clinical Supervisor*, *33*(1), 63–81. https://doi.org/10.1080/07325223.2014.918006

Beddoe, L., & Davys, A. (2016). *Challenges in professional supervision: Current themes and models for practice*. London: Jessica Kingsley Publishers.

Beddoe, L., Davys, A., & Adamson, C. (2014). "Never trust anybody who says 'I don't need supervision'": Practitioners beliefs about social worker resilience. *Practice (Birmingham, England)*, *26*(2), 113–130. https://doi.org/10.1080/09503153.2014.896888

Berger, R., & Quiros, L. (2016). Best practices for training trauma-informed practitioners: Supervisors' voice. *Traumatology*, *22*(2), 145–154. https://doi.org/10.1037/trm0000076

Davys, A., & Beddoe, L. (2010). *Best practice in professional supervision: A guide for the helping professions*. London, England: Jessica Kingsley.

Goddard, C., & Hunt, S. (2011). The complexities of caring for child protection workers: The contexts of practice and supervision. *Journal of Social Work Practice*, *25*(4), 413–432. https://doi.org/0.1080/02650533.2011.626644

Graham, J. (2012). Cognitive behavioural therapy for occupational trauma: A systematic literature review exploring the effects of occupational trauma and the existing CBT support pathways and interventions for staff working within mental healthcare including allied professions. *Cognitive Behaviour Therapist*, *5*(1), 24–45. https://doi.org/10.1017/S1754470X12000025

Hunt, S., Goddard, C., Cooper, J., Littlechild, B., & Wild, J. (2016). "If I feel like this, how does the child feel?" Child protection workers, supervision, management and organisational responses to parental violence. *Journal of Social Work Practice*, *30*(1), 5–24. https://doi.org/10.1080/02650533.2015.1073145

Kouzes, J., & Posner, B. (2016). Leading in cynical times. *Journal of Management Inquiry*, *14*(4), 357–364. https://doi.org/10.1177/1056492605280221

Little, M., Baker, T., & Jinks, A. (2018). A qualitative evaluation of community nurses' experiences of child safeguarding supervision. *Child Abuse Review*, *27*(2), 150–157. http://dx.doi.org/10.1002/car.2493

Manthorpe, J., Moriarty, J., Hussein, S., Stevens, M., & Sharpe, E. (2015). Content and purpose of supervision in social work practice in England: Views of newly qualified social workers, managers and directors. *British Journal of Social Work*, *45*(1), 52–68. https://doi.org/10.1093/bjsw/bct102

McCrae, J., Scannapieco, M., & Obermann, A. (2015). Retention and job satisfaction of child welfare supervisors. *Children and Youth Services Review*, *59*, 171–176. https://doi.org/10.1016/j.childyouth.2015.11.011

McPherson, L., Frederico, M., & McNamara, P. (2016). Safety as a fifth dimension in supervision: Stories from the frontline. *Australian Social Work*, *69*(1), 67–79. https://doi.org/10.1080/0312407X.2015.1024265

Oates, F. (2019). You are not allowed to tell: Organisational culture as a barrier for child protection workers seeking assistance for traumatic stress symptomology. *Children Australia*, *44*(2), 84–90. https://doi.org/10.1017/cha.2019.12

Pack, M. (2015). "Unsticking the stuckness": A qualitative study of the clinical supervisory needs of early-career health social workers. *British Journal of Social Work*, *45*(6), 1821–1836. https://doi.org/10.1093/bjsw/bcu069

Radey, M., & Stanley, L. (2018). "Hands on" versus "empty": Supervision experiences of frontline child welfare workers. *Children and Youth Services Review*, *91*, 128–136. https://doi.org/10.1016/j.childyouth.2018.05.037

Rankine, M. (2019). The internal/external debate: The tensions within social work supervision. *Aotearoa New Zealand Social Work*, *31*(3), 32–45. https://doi.org/10.11157/anzswj-vol31iss3id646

Regehr, C. (2018). *Stress, trauma, and decision-making for social workers*. New York: Columbia University Press.

Whinghter, L. J., Cunningham, C. J. L., Wang, M., & Burnfield, J. L. (2008). The moderating role of goal orientation in the workload-frustration relationship. *Journal of Occupational Health Psychology*, *13*(3), 283–291. https://doi.org/10.1037/1076-8998.13.3.283

Wilkins, D., Forrester, D., & Grant, L. (2017). What happens in child and family social work supervision? *Child & Family Social Work*, *22*(2), 942–951. https://doi.org/10.1111/cfs.12314

# Part two Trauma-informed principles underpinning the TISS model

## Introduction

In the introduction chapter, I briefly outlined what trauma was to establish a shared understanding of the concept. In this chapter, I will explore in more depth what trauma is specifically in the context of occupational trauma exposure that impacts practitioners working in trauma-laden environments with at-risk children and their families. I will then detail the six trauma-informed principles, namely, safety; trustworthiness and transparency; peer support, collaboration and mutuality; empowerment, voice and choice; and cultural, historical and gender considerations, in the context of the TISS model. Activities in the form of reflective questions are woven throughout the chapter to give an opportunity to consider how the trauma-informed principles in the context of the TISS model could inform the development of a practitioner's own TISS plan.

## What is trauma?

Revisiting the definition of trauma outlined in previous chapters, the Substance Abuse and Mental Health Services Administration (SAMHSA) defines trauma to be:

> Individual trauma results from an event, series of events or set of circumstances that is experienced by an individual as physically or emotionally harmful or life threatening and that has lasting adverse effects on the individual's functioning and mental, physical, social, emotional or spiritual wellbeing.
>
> (SAMHSA, 2014, p. 7)

Trauma is a normal reaction to an abnormal set of circumstances and is experienced as a persistent threat, either real or perceived (Dickson, 2017; Regehr, 2018). The experience of trauma presents as a complex mix of physiological, psychological, and environmental elements

DOI: 10.4324/9781003515371-3

(Regehr, 2018). Therefore, successful treatment must address all of these elements. Assessing need and implementing interventions to meet presenting needs is a core skill set for any practitioner working with at-risk children and their families across varying practice settings. However, when it comes to our own experience of occupational trauma, the process seems less straightforward.

## The experience of primary trauma in an occupational context

In my first book about the TISS model, I wrote about the experience of primary trauma amongst those practitioners working with at-risk children and their families. There is a strong focus in the research literature on the experience of vicarious and secondary trauma, which is important; however, the primary trauma experience often gets overlooked. Below, I have included excerpts from my first book on the TISS model about the practitioner experience of primary trauma. I have included them to normalise the experience. For many of us, myself included, who experience primary trauma in the workplace and resulting symptomology, it can feel like you are the only one impacted. This can be extremely isolating and not conducive to successfully navigating through and ultimately resolving problematic symptomology. Mary* shared an experience of primary trauma during a research interview with me about a young child that she had been working with, who had recently been removed from his family:

> *He started smashing his face into the wall repeatedly and just screaming. By this stage, he was starting to bleed at the nose . . . there's blood going everywhere . . . the scariest part. He's four.*
>
> *(Mary)*

She had conflicted feelings about the incident due to the young age of the child and feeling that she should not have been impacted by what happened because working with traumatised children is part of the job.

Parental threats of, and actual violence, are the most common sources of occupational traumatic stress exposure experienced by practitioners working with at-risk children and their families. Hunt et al. (2016) conducted a large study with 590 child welfare practitioners exploring their experience of parental violence. Hunt et al. (2016) reported that approximately half had indicated that they had had negative experiences with aggressive parents and caregivers in the past six months; 61% had indicated being threatened in the past six months; 32% stated they had been threatened three or more times in the same period. These acts of violence included physical assaults, being denied access to exits, death threats, bomb threats, threats to harm own children and pets as well as stalking and being spat at.

In my own research (Oates, 2018, 2023), practitioners shared similar experiences to those practitioners in Hunt et al.'s study. I shared their experiences in my first book; however, I will share them again below to demonstrate how common these occurrences are:

> *I remember once me and another case worker actually had to lock ourselves in a room with another [child] client in the service because they [child client] were just going crazy and smashing the place and throwing chairs and threatening everybody. We're trying to ring the police on the phone in this room.*
>
> – *Sarah*

> *It got to the point where he was standing in front of the back door preventing us from leaving. The Police had to talk to him through the back door to convince him to let us out.*
>
> – *Alice*

> *Went to do a [family] contact and was physically assaulted by the father, he shoved me into a [large hard object].*
>
> – *Mary*

> *I walked out of the office with a colleague for lunch – I had forgotten to take my ID tags off – a woman approached me, screamed that I was 'one of them' pointing to my office and then pushed me really hard. I have never seen her before – I have no idea who she was – I was so shocked I couldn't move or say anything – everyone in the street was looking at me.*
>
> – *Andrea*

More extreme examples of client violence leading to practitioners being seriously injured and in some instances losing their lives exist however I have chosen not to include them. While these incidents occur, they are not the norm. Holding these extreme examples as the benchmark for practitioners being 'allowed' to be significantly affected by client threats and violence is not helpful and fosters a culture of minimisation. The culture of minimisation within this field of practice acts as a barrier to practitioners seeking assistance when they start to experience occupational traumatic stress symptomology. This will be explored in more detail in this and subsequent chapters.

## Secondary and vicarious trauma, compassion fatigue and burnout

Practitioners working with at-risk children and their families are also exposed to secondary and vicarious trauma, compassion fatigue and burnout. There is consensus that practitioners working in trauma-laden environments with client groups that have experienced trauma are at much higher risk of developing symptomology (Bober & Regehr, 2005; Bride, 2007; Devilly et al., 2009; Fink-Samnick, 2022; Harrison & Westwood, 2009; Jankoski, 2010). Exposure to secondary and vicarious trauma is discussed in the literature as an inherent part of working with at-risk children and their families (Levy & Poertner, 2014; Munro, 2010; Wise, 2017).

### Vicarious and secondary trauma

The term vicarious trauma was originally defined by Pearlman and Saakvitne (1995) as 'the cumulative transformation in the inner experience of the therapist that comes about as a result of empathic engagement with the client's traumatic material' (p. 31). Vicarious and secondary trauma are often used interchangeably in the literature, as they have common characteristics. Both have the ability to negatively impact the psychological wellbeing of practitioners (Williams et al., 2012); shift a person's feeling of internal and external safety (Regehr, 2018); and cause symptomology like decreases in motivation and effectiveness in the workplace (Abassary & Goodrich, 2014). Regehr (2018) groups the symptomologies of vicarious trauma experienced by practitioners into three core areas, namely, intrusion, arousal and avoidance (p. 8). The intrusion domain is characterised by Regehr (2018) to include symptomologies like intrusive thoughts and sleep disturbances like nightmares as well as distress when recalling events that have been traumatic. Within the arousal domain, one could expect to experience hypervigilance, concentration difficulties, behavioural outbursts or interrupted sleep. Of the avoidance category, Regehr (2018) cites that practitioners may manage their distressing symptomology "through numbing, detachment, loss of memory regarding a traumatic event, and/or efforts to avoid thoughts or stimuli that are reminiscent of the event" (p. 8).

### Compassion fatigue and burnout

In the research literature, compassion fatigue and burnout are often used interchangeably due to the similarities in symptomology which can include emotional and physical exhaustion, reduced job satisfaction, anxiety and depression as well as a decreased capacity for empathy (Figley, 2012; Hinds & Giardino, 2020; Regehr, 2018). Practitioners experiencing compassion fatigue can become desensitised to the experiences of clients and their needs, which can result in an impaired ability to make sound evidence-based decisions, increasing the likelihood of mistakes (Figley, 2012; Hinds & Giardino, 2020; Regehr, 2018). Other behavioural indicators in practitioners who may be experiencing compassion fatigue include irritability, negativity, lower levels of concentration, persistent tiredness, or depersonalisation or minimisation of suffering, both in a general sense and in regard to clients (Berzoff & Kita, 2010; Geoffrion et al., 2015).

In relation to burnout, McFadden (2020) argues that professionals working with at-risk children and their families are at increased risk due to the inherent nature of the work including the occupational environment that work occurs in. Practitioners working with this client group contend with additional stressors including unrealistic workloads, onerous paperwork including preparations for court matters, austerity measures limiting quality interventions, onerous media attention and negative perceptions by the public all within an environment that is chronically under-resourced and under-staffed (Geoffrion et al., 2015; Hunt et al., 2016; McFadden, 2020; Oates, 2019; Radey & Wilke, 2023; Regehr, 2018).

## Dosage–response relationship

Not all instances of trauma result in the problematic experience of traumatic stress symptomology. The correlation between the amount and/or severity of trauma endured and the ongoing experience of problematic symptomology that won't resolve is referred to in the research literature as the dosage–response relationship. It is difficult to determine whether or not there is a correlation between the amount of trauma experienced and the likelihood of ongoing problematic symptomology, as there are conflicting and contradictory findings in the research literature. As an example, Meyer et al. (2012) found in their study with firefighters, no correlation between frequency of exposure and experience of traumatic stress symptomology. Conversely, Behnke et al. (2020) found in a review of multiple studies exploring the dosage-response connection, that the higher the number of traumatic incidents experienced by 'trauma-exposed' professions like emergency services personnel, the more likely the development of traumatic stress symptomology to be (p. 2). Regehr (2018) found in relation to social workers' exposure to trauma while undertaking their occupational duties that the nature of the trauma was not a predictor of ongoing traumatic stress symptomology but rather a 'complex interaction between the individual, the organisation, and the societal environment' to be a more definitive measurement (p. 15). There is some consensus in the research literature about what factors may predispose a person to experience ongoing traumatic stress symptomology after experiencing a trauma or series of traumas. Meyer et al. (2012) found that factors like self-blame and perceived social and organisational support were more accurate predictors of ongoing clinically significant symptomology. Behnke et al. (2020) found that the history of childhood maltreatment was a significant factor that may predispose people working in trauma-exposed professions to ongoing traumatic stress symptomologies while undertaking occupational duties.

Despite conflicting research findings regarding the dosage-response relationship, there is some common agreement in relation to factors that may lead to positive resolution of trauma-related stress symptomologies for practitioners. These factors include perceived social support and connection and satisfaction within the role and workplace. There is research literature that suggests that external environmental factors like an empathetic work environment including an attuned supervisor, manageable workload, supervision and peer support, are more likely to result in the resolution of traumatic stress symptomologies over a longer-term period (McFadden et al., 2015; Regehr, 2018). These findings are significant as they support that what happens after a traumatic event may be more significant than the individual circumstances present for a person prior to a traumatic event taking place. The TISS model incorporates these findings by providing scaffolding around the practitioner rather than solely relying on an organisational response or by placing the responsibility on the individual impacted practitioner to tend to their own needs.

## Occupational trauma exposure

In an occupational context, Graham (2012) defines occupational trauma as 'the psychological effects of trauma directly attributable to occupational activity' (p.25). There is agreement in the literature that although the scope of trauma exposure for individuals is narrowed to events occurring while undertaking one's occupational duties, the negative symptomology experienced are similar to trauma symptomology experienced by the general population (Graham, 2012; Rubino et al., 2009). Trauma-related impacts on individuals are grouped into three key categories, namely psychological or somatic, physical and social (Behnke et al., 2020; Graham, 2012). Psychological or somatic effects include internalised shame, negative self-image and esteem, features of depression and anxiety and exhaustion emotionally (Rubino et al., 2009; Behnke et al., 2020; Oates, 2019). Effects attributed to physical impacts of trauma include insomnia and other sleep disturbances, nausea and other digestive complaints, fatigue and overall poorer health (Eidelson et al., 2003; McFarlane & Bryant, 2007; Pyevich et al., 2003). The social impacts were outlined in the literature to include negative disruptions in family life and other relationships an increase in maladaptive coping strategies like alcohol and other substance misuse and withdrawal from social interactions (Graham, 2012; Oates, 2019; Rantanen et al., 2011).

## Examples of occupational trauma exposure

It is common for practitioners not to identify with the concept of occupational trauma exposure, often dismissing it as part of the job or as extreme situations that happen to a small proportion of people working with at-risk children and their families. I have included the three case studies below because they are not on the extreme end of the spectrum. They are examples of day to day occurrences in the professional lives of practitioners who work in trauma-laden environments with at-risk children and their families. The persistent exposure to violence, including threats of violence, as well as distressed children and young people, leaves the nervous system of practitioners constantly activated and therefore at increased risk of experiencing occupational traumatic stress symptomology:

> *I met with a mother to tell her that we were taking a guardianship order on her daughter until she was 18 years of age. She became extremely angry, grabbed a metal can of whiteboard cleaner that was in the room and threw it in my direction. It missed me but hit the wall behind where I was sitting. It left a large dint. She stormed out. I felt alert but then had to move on to the next parent meeting. Its part of the job I guess.*
>
> – *Lauren*

> *I had to investigate allegations of that a foster care and her adult children had physically harmed and neglected a five year old girl – SM. When I got there the foster carer wasn't there but her adult daughters were and had already packed all SM's belongings. SM was sitting next to her bags staring into space. The adult daughters told me that the devil was in that girl and that she was no longer welcome in her mother's home. I told them that I would be taking SM and that I would arrange another time to interview them and their mother as SM was the current priority. My colleague and I put SM in the car and drove to a nearby park. Over snacks, SM told us some of the things that had*

*been happening to her in her foster placement. Things like the adult daughters washing her mouth out with soap, swearing at her and slapping her when she 'misbehaved'. SM told us that the foster mother was often not home and sometimes she would be gone for days at a time leaving the adult daughters to look after her. Sometimes they made her meals and sometimes they didn't. Sometimes they made sure she showered and brushed her teeth and sometimes they didn't. Sometimes they took her to child care and sometimes they didn't. All through the interview SM didn't cry, she just told us the facts as she remembered them with a flat affect. When she finished, I told her that we would be going to a new foster home. Immediately her demeanour changed. She became instantly heightened, screaming that she wouldn't go. She ran to the car and started hitting and kicking the doors, windows and seats. I got in the back seat with her which heightened her even more. I tried everything I knew to calm her. Nothing worked. The more I tried, the more heightened she became. I had no idea what to do. My colleague said we should drive to the new foster placement as it was only a few minutes away. It was getting dark. I buckled SM in as best I could getting kicked and hit while doing so. When I think of the situation now, I can still feel the ringing in my ears from the screaming. I feel my chest tightening just thinking about how I let her down. She must have been terrified.*

*– Michelle*

*I went to a rural property to serve court documents to a parent. She had a very large, very angry dog that came pelting down the dirt driveway. I shoved the documents in the letter box and ran back to the car as fast as I could. I was terrified. Thinking about it makes my heart pound. It happened 6 years ago.*

*– Yvette*

## Symptomology of occupational traumatic stress in the workplace

Above, I have explored the physical and somatic symptoms as well as the social impacts of trauma. I will now explore the presentation of occupational traumatic stress symptomology in the context of the workplace. As previously mentioned, commonly attributed symptomology can include sleep disturbances including insomnia or nightmares, feeling tired, irritable or unable to relax, gastrointestinal upset or changes in appetite, increased alcohol or substance use or reliance on other maladaptive coping strategies, lack of ability to find joy in previously enjoyable tasks and withdrawal from relationships including professional relationships. Some uncommonly attributed symptomologies can include persistent intrusive thoughts, difficulty making or trusting decisions, feelings of doom &/or despair about the future, difficulty trusting self &/or others, obsessive thinking not related to work, that is, health concerns or insignificant details of events.

Practitioners experiencing occupational traumatic stress symptomology are often not the easiest of colleagues to be around. They can present in a constant state of negativity or aggression, and they could be distracted or completely withdrawn. Practitioners struggling with occupational traumatic stress can exhibit behavioural presentations like non-performance & absenteeism, avoidance, withdrawal and/or aggression, lack of ability to take responsibility and/or externalising blame, engaging in frequent negative gossip, venting or being overly critical about colleagues, managers or the organisation, difficulty separating work and home life including oversharing and the impaired ability for self-reflection. The traumatised brain can detect threats where there are none, leading struggling practitioners to turn away from formal and informal supports. Practitioners experiencing symptomology of occupational traumatic stress can often become subject to performance management measures, given these behavioural presentations create further disconnection from supports and alienation from the workgroup.

## Occupational trauma exposure – no response is celebrated as resilience

Exposure to occupational trauma while working in trauma-laden environments is an occupational inevitability; however, organisations struggle to acknowledge that the symptomology of occupational traumatic stress is a normal reaction to abnormally high and persistent levels of threat. When practitioners begin to display behavioural patterns consistent with occupational traumatic stress, organisations struggle to manage these presentations, resulting often in practitioners being performance managed, ostracised by their peers or labelled as not resilient enough to cope with the work. Culturally, there is great incentive for practitioners not to seek assistance when they start to experience symptomology that won't resolve. A lack of reaction to extreme situations and/or persistent threats of or actual violence is celebrated culturally within trauma-laden occupational environments as 'resilience' which again provides a strong incentive for practitioners not to seek assistance or to deny that they may be struggling when asked if they are doing ok.

A lack of response to traumatic events can be considered a trauma response. It can be our brain's way of coping, similar to the presentations practitioners see in the children and families they work with. To demonstrate how a lack of response can indeed be a trauma response rather than a demonstration of resilience, I will share two examples.

The first example from my own experience as a practitioner was a young person I worked with who presented with chronic self-injurious behaviour. She would often need hospital treatment as a result of her injuries. One day, she was released from the hospital with heavy bandaging protecting extensive stitching. As I was sitting with her talking, she had managed to get into the bandaging and was picking the stitches out of her wounds, resulting in extensive bleeding. I chose this example to share because on reflection, at the time I had no response to the situation. This was a young woman that I had become extremely fond of and given her risk and vulnerability, would see multiple times per week. And still, I had no reaction other than thinking we probably should go back to the hospital and would I have time to eat before my next appointment. Reflecting back on this situation, I feel a disconnect between how I responded then and how I would respond now. I also reflect on the fact that this was one of many blood-related occurrences I experienced while working in statutory child protection. Some years later, I was diagnosed with a blood phobia. The origin of this condition was most likely occupational trauma exposure as I didn't have this presentation prior to undertaking statutory child protection work. This is an example that demonstrates that trauma-related symptomologies can start to be experienced some time after an incident has occurred. A lack of response at the time is not a demonstration that practitioners will be ok post-exposure.

The second example to demonstrate that a lack of response to occupational trauma exposure is actually a symptom of trauma is a story shared with me by a stranger at a wedding. I met a woman who told me she had spent 30 years working is the community housing sector. At the time, I was working with organisations that delivered housing and homelessness services and I told her that I was shocked to learn how often practitioners in that sector find clients who are deceased. She told me that it was a common occurrence, one that she had experienced multiple times. She told me that it never impacted her and that it was just part of the job. She then told me that about ten years earlier, she entered a community housing property located in a high-rise apartment building to do a routine inspection. She found the tenant sitting in a lounge chair. They had been deceased for several months. She told me that every day since, when she drives past a multilevel apartment building, she wonders how many dead people are in there rotting away.

It would be easy on the face of these situations for line supervisors and managers to assess that the reaction of the practitioner is a demonstration of resilience. Both these examples demonstrate that no response at the time of an incident is not an indication that a practitioner won't go on to experience occupational traumatic stress symptomology that may become challenging to manage. This evidences the importance of scaffolded supervision models that are responsive to practitioner needs rather than a one-size-fits-all approach.

## The resilience myth

Resilience of the practitioner is strongly focused on in the research literature as a key factor in a practitioner's ability to move through occupational trauma exposure and related symptomology. However, focusing solely on the perceived resilience of practitioners as a predicting factor of ongoing practitioner wellness in the face of occupational trauma exposure fails to acknowledge that individual practitioners are small pieces in large multifaceted complex systems. Practitioner wellbeing must be viewed within a systems context, not just through the prism of individual responsibility. Strategies that support the internalising of occupational traumatic stress symptomologies by practitioners as a failure in their ability to have and maintain resilience is not an appropriate response by organisations, line supervisors and managers or peers. They will also not be effective in improving practitioner wellbeing or retention.

## Impact on organisational service delivery

The quality of service delivery being negatively impacted by practitioners experiencing a lack of support is noted in the research literature. Factors contributing to this are increased practitioner absenteeism (Parks & Steelman, 2008) and an impaired ability to manage the demands of their workload (Hecht & Boies, 2009; Oates, 2019) including their ability to make sound decisions (Regehr, 2018) and the ability to recall critical information when needed (Leblanc, 2009). Regehr (2018) has written extensively on how exposure to occupational trauma impacts a practitioner's decision making capacity. Regehr (2018) states that:

> professional decision making can be affected by both acute stress related to the current situation and traumatic stress responses to previous encounters. Individuals in acutely stressful situations may experience selective attention, focusing particularly on threat stimuli with limited ability to consider other factors. Acute stress impacts computational capacity, requiring individuals to rely more heavily on heuristics as deliberative cognitive processing and decision-making capacities are constricted
>
> (pp. 13–14).

The lack of quality support and supervision available to practitioners working with at-risk children and families may in fact increase the risk to this cohort.

## What is trauma informed?

The term trauma informed in now ubiquitous in the human, social and health services landscape and dominates many organisational policy and procedure documents. In my experience when this happens, the meaning can get watered down, weakening the impact of the practice. Before we move into the trauma informed principles in the context of the TISS model, I thought it might be useful to re-visit the concept of trauma informed in a general sense. Wall et al. (2016) describe trauma-informed care in its simplest form to be 'a framework for human service delivery that is based on knowledge and understanding of how trauma affects people's lives and their service needs' (p. 9). Applying this definition to the work a practitioner undertakes with at-risk children and their families, practitioners would assess the presenting situation based on their knowledge of how trauma can impact a person's experience of the world including their ability to engage in meaningful service delivery. With that knowledge set in mind, a practitioner would then holistically craft a service intervention response that is unique to that presenting set of circumstances. The same definition applies to trauma informed service delivery within an organisational context, that is, organisational processes need to be informed by the knowledge and understanding of how the experience of trauma (individual, collective and historical) impacts the group the organisation is funded to provide services to.

Whether in an individual or organisational context, SAMHSA (2014) defines a trauma informed approach to service delivery to be:

> A programme, organisation or system that is trauma-informed realises the widespread impact of trauma and understands potential paths for recovery; recognises the signs and symptoms of trauma in clients, families, staff and others involved with the system and responds by fully integrating knowledge about trauma into policies, procedures and practices and seeks to actively resist re-traumatisation.
>
> (p. 9)

The above is consistent with the work of Regehr (2018), who argues organisations should shoulder some of the responsibility to mitigate the inherent risks to practitioners that work in trauma-laden environments while delivering services to at-risk children and their families. Regehr (2018) states that organisations need to 'take responsibility for reducing exposure to the extent possible, for mitigating the impacts of stress and trauma exposure, and for providing services when individual social workers are suffering' (p. 16).

## The six trauma informed principles in the context of the TISS model

In the introduction chapter, I briefly introduced the six trauma informed principles, namely, safety; trustworthiness and transparency; peer support, collaboration and mutuality; empowerment, voice and choice; and cultural, historical and gender considerations, that underpin the TISS model and the context in which they are applied. I will now discuss the trauma informed principles in the context of the TISS model in more depth. After each principle is discussed, an activity will follow that will assist readers with preparing for the development of their own TISS plan.

## Trauma informed principle one: *safety*

The key finding in the research literature about what determines a successful supervisory relationship for practitioners is the creation and maintenance of safety. For this reason, the safety principle is the most important of the six trauma informed principles as it is foundation of all of them. The principle of safety is threaded through the remaining five principles tying them all together. Without the feeling of safety, the principles cannot work in harmony with each other. The safety principle also underpins the four core pillars in the TISS model which will be explored in greater detail in subsequent chapters. The principles of safety in the context of the TISS model refers to what the practitioner needs to achieve the internal feeling of safety. Without the practitioner having a sense of safety within their support and supervision arrangements, their capacity to engage effectively in such arrangements will be compromised. I acknowledge that thinking about support and supervision from this lens is not congruent with how traditional models of supervision typically tend to be delivered especially when a practitioner's line supervisor or manager is the one delivering it. Given this, practitioners may need time and assistance to think through exactly what it is they might need to achieve safety. Practitioners may need to ask themselves questions like:

- What do I need to feel safe in my supervisory (line manager) relationship?
- What behaviours do I need my supervisor to demonstrate?
- What behaviours would I demonstrate if I was feeling safe and secure in my supervisory relationship?

- If there was a concern about my work, how would I want this addressed in a way that maintains safety?

A key area to address within this principle is how one might manage their support and supervision needs if there is a threat to achieving the sense of safety. Threats may present in several ways. It could be that a practitioner is mistrustful of their supervisor. It might be onerous work demands or a hostile organisational culture. The TISS model allows a practitioner to explore alternatives to achieving safety even if there are threats present within their support and supervision arrangements.

## Reflective activity

- What are the barriers to me achieving a sense of safety?
- What do I need to safety plan for these threats and/or barriers?
- Are there other ways I can achieve safety if my relationship with my line supervisor feels unsafe?

Notes:

## Trauma informed principle two: *trustworthiness and transparency*

The principle of trustworthiness and transparency in the context of the TISS model relates to the process of support and supervision arrangements inclusive of the supervisory relationship. The research literature indicates that many practitioners are suspicious of supervision citing concerns about it being used as a covert performance management tool or to surveil practitioners (Beddoe & Davys, 2016). Because of this suspicion, that the supervision process is used for surveillance and quasi-performance management, practitioners either avoid attending supervision with their line manager or they only engage in a superficial way leaving their wellbeing and professional development needs largely unmet. This principle calls for practitioners and line supervisors to come to an agreement about what supervision is, what it isn't, and what the process will be if a practitioner's work performance requires addressing. As mentioned previously, an effective supervisory relationship is cited in the research literature as a protective factor present that facilitates a practitioner's movement through occupational stress symptomology (Beddoe et al., 2014; Berger & Quiros, 2016; McPherson et al., 2016). Therefore, it is critical that trustworthiness and transparency is achieved within a practitioner's support and supervision arrangements.

I acknowledge that a conversation about what performance management might look like when no performance concerns are present is a deviation from the usual practice within traditional supervision models. However, the research literature indicates as previously mentioned, that practitioner fear of supervision being used for this purpose is a barrier to practitioners engaging in a meaningful way in the process. The TISS model, using this trauma-informed principle, facilitates the opportunity to have a professionally mature conversation about what performance management would look like so that this fear can be somewhat addressed.

### Reflective activity

Questions a practitioner might ask include:

- If I were to be performance managed, what would the process look like?
- How would our supervision sessions be used in that process?
- What kind of communication would I expect to receive?
- Would the wellbeing and professional development portion of supervision be outsourced to manage any perceived or actual conflict?

Questions like these being to lay the foundations of transparency, increasing a practitioner's capacity to more effectively engage in the supervision process and strengthen the supervisory relationship.

Notes:

## Trauma informed principle three: *peer support*

The peer support principle in the context of the TISS model refers to the inclusion of peer support as part of a practitioner's support and supervision arrangements. Peer support is critical to practitioner wellbeing while working with at-risk children and their families. Anyone who has worked with at-risk children and their families knows that we are drawn to each other. Talking with others who share our experiences creates a sense of belonging and there is comfort and often a sense of safety within that. Interactions with other practitioners in this field allow us to have frank and open conversations about the work and the environment that work is undertaken in. This sense of community can be very therapeutic especially in relation to managing occupational traumatic stress.

Like the first two principles, peer support models must also have a safety focus for them to be beneficial. Not all peer support is safe, and practitioners must exercise caution around the disclosure of personal information that they wish not to be shared outside of the peer support context. In the context of the TISS model, some structure around what peer support is, what it isn't, and what the boundaries are is advised. Further, having some structure to the peer support element within a practitioner's support and supervision arrangements assist a practitioner's organisation to view this as a legitimate source of support rather than a paid opportunity to get together and gossip with your work friends.

It is my view that peer support is critical and is something that I engage in regularly. However, it must be noted that an overreliance on peer support can also be detrimental. The practice environment and the lack of quality and responsive support and supervision within organisations, can create a culture of overreliance on peer support. Peer support cannot be the only source of support practitioners rely on. Peers may be experiencing similar struggles with occupational traumatic stress symptomology, reducing their ability to identify the key indicators in others. Peer support is a critical element, but it should not be the only element in a practitioner's support and supervision arrangements.

## Reflective activity

- What does good peer support look like to me? Structured? Semi-structured? Free-range?
- Who should be included in my peer support arrangements? What is their role?

Notes:

## Trauma informed principle four: *collaboration and mutuality*

The collaboration and mutuality principle in the context of the TISS model relates to the partnership element that is required to have an effective support and supervision arrangement. The TISS model is practitioner-centred, meaning that the practitioner is an equal contributing participant in their support and supervision (TISS plan) arrangements. The student and expert dynamic within traditional supervision models is challenged by this principle which shifts the focus to a collaboration between equals – the outcome sought being the effective support of the practitioner. Now it would be naïve to think that a shifting of focus also shifts the power dynamics within the supervisory relationship. It is important to openly acknowledge these power dynamics and work towards a mutually acceptable arrangement.

Job satisfaction is cited in the research literature as contributing to a practitioner's decision to stay in the field of working with at-risk children and their families (Beddoe et al., 2014; Berger & Quiros, 2016; Hunt et al., 2016; Regehr, 2018). A collaboration focus within a practitioner's support and supervision arrangements can be a vehicle to assist with an increase in a practitioner's feeling of job satisfaction. How can the TISS team work together to meet the professional development needs of practitioners? What additional opportunities for growth can be identified through such a collaboration?

### Reflective activity

- What does job satisfaction look like to me? What does it feel like?
- What would I need in my TISS plan to assist me to build on my sense of job satisfaction?

Notes:

## Trauma-informed principle five: *empowerment, voice and choice*

The empowerment, voice and choice principle in the context of the TISS model refers to the practitioner's ability to fully and effectively participate in a support and supervision arrangement that contributes to maintaining their wellbeing and professional development. Practitioners must be empowered to identify their needs and be fully involved in what it would take to have those needs met. As practitioners, we know that people are the experts in their own experiences and will often have the solutions to presenting problems. The same is true for practitioners. However, it must be noted that the TISS model which is practitioner-centred, is a deviation from some traditional models of supervision which the majority of practitioners would be familiar. Practitioners may need to be empowered to explore what their needs actually are, as this may be the first time they have considered this in the context of the TISS model. Similarly, the autonomy to confidently voice what they need and then to choose how to meet those identified needs may be a first-time experience. Empowering practitioners to voice what their wellbeing and professional development needs are and then choosing how to have those needs best met will also contribute to an increase in job satisfaction. As previously explored, job satisfaction is frequently cited in the research literature as a critical element in retaining practitioners who work with at-risk children and their families.

Of course the caveat to the above is that not all supervisory relationships or organisational cultures are characterised by the conditions needed to have this element fully realised. In situations like these I would recommend focusing on the other parts of the TISS plan where you can have more autonomy. This might look like your choice of external supervisor, the professional development activities you engage in or the peers you interact with.

## Reflective activity

Questions that might be considered as part of this principle include:

- How do I feel when I have had my voice recognised in relation to my wellbeing and professional development needs?
- Do I need assistance to have my voice recognised? Accommodations?
- What if I can't voice what I need?

Notes:

## Trauma informed principle six: *cultural, historical and gender considerations*

The cultural, historical, and gender considerations principle in the context of the TISS model explores sources of support that a practitioner identifies with. As an example, a female identifying practitioner may wish to receive supports from other female identifying professionals. This may be to reduce interruption from patriarchal oppression (real or perceived) and creates an opportunity for a practitioner to engage more fully with their supports. Similarly, a practitioner may wish to engage in supports with another practitioner of the same cultural or language background, again to remove barriers to participation and increase the effectiveness of support and supervision arrangements. Members of the queer community, First Nation's people, people belonging to minority cultural and faith backgrounds have all been persecuted historically for their identity. Having someone from the same or similar background to oneself may increase a practitioner's internal sense of safety, therefore increasing their capacity to engage with support and supervision. Similarly, a practitioner may want to avoid having someone from a similar background to their own for a myriad of reasons – this must also be respected.

This principle also encourages practitioners to explore other elements that they may wish to have considered as part of their support and supervision arrangements. This may include an external supervisor (or other source of support) who shares a history of trauma, is neurodivergent, is first in family or other similar presentations they find relevant to their own needs.

### Reflective activity

Questions to explore might include:

- Would a supervisor (or other source of support) assist me to create a sense of safety in my support and supervision arrangements?
- If yes, what would that look like?

Notes:

## Working with the trauma informed principles to formulate your own TISS plan

Now that I have explored the six trauma-informed principles in the context of the TISS model, I would like to offer some concluding thoughts. As mentioned, safety is the principle that binds all the elements together and allows them to work in harmony. When a practitioner feels a sense of safety within their support and supervision arrangements, it increases their capacity to engage effectively in supports and work through occupational traumatic stress symptomology when experienced. How safety is achieved must be practitioner-led. This cannot be defined by line supervisors, managers or organisations.

## Chapter summary

In this chapter, I have discussed the general concept of trauma, what occupational trauma looks like, and explored primary and vicarious trauma, compassion fatigue, and burnout. Then the six trauma-informed principles, namely, safety; trustworthiness and transparency; peer support, collaboration and mutuality; empowerment, voice and choice; and cultural, historical and gender considerations were explored in the context of the TISS model. Reflective activities were woven throughout the chapter as prompts to assist practitioners to start preparing for the formulation and implementation of their own TISS plan. Safety was established as the foundational principle and one that is critical to achieving effective support and supervision arrangements for practitioners.

## References

Abassary, C., & Goodrich, K. M. (2014). Attending to crisis-based supervision for counselors: The CARE model of crisis-based supervision. *The Clinical Supervisor*, *33*(1), 63–81. https://doi.org/10.1080/07325223.2014.918006

Beddoe, L., & Davys, A. (2016). *Challenges in professional supervision: Current themes and models for practice*. London: Jessica Kingsley Publishers.

Beddoe, L., Davys, A., & Adamson, C. (2014). "Never trust anybody who says 'I don't need supervision'": Practitioners beliefs about social worker resilience. *Practice (Birmingham, England)*, *26*(2), 113–130. https://doi.org/10.1080/09503153.2014.896888

Behnke, A., Rojas, R., Karabatsiakis, A., & Kolassa, I. (2020). Childhood maltreatment compromises resilience against occupational trauma exposure: A retrospective study among emergency medical service personnel. *Child Abuse & Neglect*, *99*, 104248–104248. https://doi.org/10.1016/j.chiabu.2019.104248

Berger, R., & Quiros, L. (2016). Best practices for training trauma-informed practitioners: Supervisors' voice. *Traumatology*, *22*(2), 145–154. https://doi.org/10.1037/trm0000076

Berzoff, J., & Kita, E. (2010). Compassion fatigue and countertransference: Two different concepts. *Clinical Social Work Journal*, *38*(3), 341–349. https://doi.org/10.1007/s10615-010-0271-8

Bober, T., & Regehr, C. (2005). Strategies for reducing secondary or vicarious trauma: Do they work? *Brief Treatment and Crisis Intervention*, *6*(1), 1–9. https://doi.org/10.1093/brief-treatment/mhj001

Bride, B. (2007). Prevalence of secondary traumatic stress among social workers. *Social Work*, *52*(1), 63–70. https://doi.org/10.1093/sw/52.1.63

Devilly, G., Wright, R., & Varker, T. (2009). Vicarious trauma, secondary traumatic stress or simply burnout? Effect of trauma therapy on mental health professionals. *Australasian Psychiatry*, *43*(4), 373–385. https://doi.org/10.1080/00048670902721079

Dickson, M. (2017). *What does trauma-informed mean? Grappling with the challenge*. http://professionals.childhood.org.au/prosody/2017/11/what-does-trauma-informed-mean/

Eidelson, R., D'Alessio, G., & Eidelson, J. (2003). The impact of September 11 on psychologists. *Professional Psychology, Research and Practice*, *34*(2), 144–150. https://doi.org/10.1037/0735-7028.34.2.144

Figley, C. (Ed.). (2012). Compassion fatigue. In *Encyclopedia of trauma: An interdisciplinary guide*. New York, NY: SAGE. doi.org/10.4135/9781452218595

Fink-Samnick, E. (2022). Collective occupational trauma, health care quality, and trauma-informed leadership: Intersections and implications. *Professional Case Management*, *27*(3), 107–123. https://doi.org/10.1097/NCM.0000000000000559

Geoffrion, S., Morselli, C., & Guay, S. (2015/2016). Rethinking compassion fatigue through the lens of professional identity: The case of child-protection workers. *Trauma, Violence & Abuse*, *17*(3), 270–283. https://doi.org/10.1177/1524838015584362

Graham, J. (2012). Cognitive behavioural therapy for occupational trauma: A systematic literature review exploring the effects of occupational trauma and the existing CBT support pathways and interventions for staff working within mental healthcare including allied professions. *Cognitive Behaviour Therapist*, *5*(1), 24–45. https://doi.org/10.1017/S1754470X12000025

Harrison, R., & Westwood, M. (2009). Preventing vicarious traumatization of mental health therapists: Identifying protective practices. *Psychotherapy: Theory, Research, Practice, Training*, *46*(2), 203–219. https://doi.org/10.1037/a0016081

Hecht, T., & Boies, K. (2009). Structure and correlates of spillover from nonwork to work: An examination of nonwork activities, well-being, and work outcomes. *Journal of Occupational Health Psychology*, *14*(4), 414–426. https://doi.org/10.1037/a0015981

Hinds, T., & Giardino, A. (2020). Compassion fatigue, burnout, and coping strategies among child-serving professionals. In *Child sexual abuse. Springer briefs in public health* (pp. 95–102). Cham: Springer. https://doi.org/10.1007/978-3-030-52549-1_4

Hunt, S., Goddard, C., Cooper, J., Littlechild, B., & Wild, J. (2016). "If I feel like this, how does the child feel?" Child protection workers, supervision, management and organisational responses to parental violence. *Journal of Social Work Practice*, *30*(1), 5–24. https://doi.org/10.1080/02650533.2015.1073145

Jankoski, J. (2010). Is vicarious trauma the culprit? A study of child welfare professionals. *Child Welfare*, *89*(6), 105–131.

Leblanc, V. R. (2009). The effects of acute stress on performance: Implications for health professions education. *Academic Medicine*, *84*(10), S25–S33. https://doi.org/10.1097/ACM.0b013e3181b37b8f

Levy, M., & Poertner, J. (2014). Development of a child welfare worker stress inventory. *Journal of Psychological Issues in Organizational Culture*, *5*(1), 7–15. https://doi:10.1002/jpoc.21134

McFadden, P. (2020). Two sides of one coin? Relationships build resilience or contribute to burnout in child protection social work: Shared perspectives from leavers and stayers in Northern Ireland. *International Social Work*, *63*(2), 164–176. https://doi.org/10.1177/0020872818788393

McFadden, P., Campbell, A., & Taylor, B. (2015). Resilience and burnout in child protection social work: Individual and organisational themes from a systematic literature review. *The British Journal of Social Work*, *45*(5), 1546–1563. https://doi.org/10.1093/bjsw/bct210

McFarlane, A., & Bryant, R. (2007). Post-traumatic stress disorder in occupational settings: Anticipating and managing the risk. *Occupational Medicine (Oxford)*, *57*, 404–410. https://doi.org/10.1093/occmed/kqm070

McPherson, L., Frederico, M., & McNamara, P. (2016). Safety as a fifth dimension in supervision: Stories from the frontline. *Australian Social Work*, *69*(1), 67–79. https://doi.org/10.1080/0312407X.2015.1024265

Meyer, E. C., Zimering, R., Daly, E., Knight, J., Kamholz, B. W., & Gulliver, S. B. (2012). Predictors of posttraumatic stress disorder and other psychological symptoms in trauma-exposed firefighters. *Psychological Services*, *9*(1), 1–15. https://doi.org/10.1037/a0026414

Munro, E. (2010). *The Munro review of child protection: Interim report – the child's journey*. London, England: Department of Education.

Oates, F. (2018). *Working for the welfare: Exploring the experiences of Indigenous child protection workers* [Doctoral dissertation, James Cook University]. https://doi.org/10.25903/5bea03dc810f3

Oates, F. (2019). You are not allowed to tell: Organisational culture as a barrier for child protection workers seeking assistance for traumatic stress symptomology. *Children Australia*, *44*(2), 84–90. https://doi.org/10.1017/cha.2019.12

Oates, F. (2023). *Trauma informed support and supervision for child protection professionals: A model for those working with children who have experienced trauma, abuse and neglect and their families* (1st ed.). Routledge. https://doi.org/10.4324/9781003026006

Parks, K., & Steelman, L. (2008). Organizational wellness programs: A meta-analysis. *Journal of Occupational Health Psychology*, *13*(1), 58–68. https://doi.org/10.1037/1076-8998.13.1.58

Pearlman, L., & Saakvitne, K. (1995). *Trauma and the therapist: Countertransference and vicarious traumatization in psychotherapy with incest survivors*. New York, NY: Norton.

Pyevich, C., Newman, E., & Daleiden, E. (2003). The relationship among cognitive schemas, job-related traumatic exposure, and post-traumatic stress disorder in journalists. *Journal of Traumatic Stress*, *16*(4), 325–328. https://doi.org/10.1023/A:1024405716529

Radey, M., & Wilke, D. J. (2023). The importance of job demands and supports: Promoting retention among child welfare workers. *Child & Adolescent Social Work Journal*, *40*(1), 57–69. https://doi.org/10.1007/s10560-021-00762-z

Rantanen, M., Mauno, S., Kinnunen, U., & Rantanen, U. (2011). Do individual coping strategies help or harm in the work–family conflict situation? Examining coping as a moderator between work–family conflict and well-being. *International Journal of Stress Management*, *18*(1), 24–48. https://doi.org/10.1037/a0022007

Regehr, C. (2018). *Stress, trauma, and decision-making for social workers*. New York: Columbia University Press.

Rubino, C., Luksyte, A., Perry, S., & Volpone, S. (2009). How do stressors lead to burnout? The mediating role of motivation. *Journal of Occupational Health Psychology*, *14*(3), 289–304. https://doi.org/10.1037/a0015284

Substance Abuse and Mental Health Services Administration. (2014). *SAMHSA's concept of trauma and guidance for a trauma informed approach*. Rockville, MD: Substance Abuse and Mental Health Services Administration.

Wall, L., Higgins, D., & Hunter, C. (2016). *Trauma-informed care in child/family welfare services (CFCA paper no. 37)*. Melbourne: Child Family Community Australia Information Exchange, Australian Institute of Family Studies.

Williams, A., Helm, H., & Clemens, E. (2012). The effect of childhood trauma, personal wellness, supervisory working alliance, and organizational factors on vicarious traumatization. *Journal of Mental Health Counseling*, *34*(2), 133–153. https://doi.org/10.17744/mehc.34.2.j3l62k872325h583

Wise, S. (2017). *Developments to strengthen systems for child protection across Australia (CFCA paper no. 44)*. Melbourne, VIC: Child Family Community Australia Information Exchange, Australian Institute of Family Studies.

# Part three Four core pillars of the TISS model

## Introduction

The TISS model is practitioner-centred, meaning the practitioner is at the core. However, individual practitioners do not exist within a silo. They are part of a complex system which includes not only themselves but the line supervisor to whom they are allocated, the organisation they work for and the local context they work in. All four of these elements must be considered when designing an individual TISS plan. Acknowledging that practitioners are located within a larger system can assist them in working through occupational distress that is rooted in a systemic context. An example of this might be when practitioners develop a sense of hopelessness working within the 'system'. In my own time working with practitioners, it is almost always the 'system' that contributes to a practitioner's decision to leave their role working with at-risk children and their families, rather than the vulnerable children and families themselves. In this chapter, we explore the four core pillars, namely, the practitioner, the line supervisor (and TISS team), the organisation and local contextualisation. Why they were included in the TISS model and how they can be applied to the development and implementation of a TISS plan will also be explored.

## The practitioner

I have the deepest respect for those practitioners who work with at-risk children and their families. The work is extremely complex and is undertaken in challenging trauma-laden environments. Practitioners are drawn to working with at-risk children and their families for several reasons. One of the common reasons is that they have a trauma background themselves. Some know what it is to struggle with circumstances not of their own making. Some know what it is to be in pain with seemingly no end in sight. All have empathy for the pain and struggle of others. It can be useful to consider why one decided

DOI: 10.4324/9781003515371-4

to work in this field. Connecting or re-connecting with the motivation that brought you to work with at-risk children and their families can give clues as to the types of supports that may be most effective preventatively as well as post the experience of occupational traumatic stress symptomology.

Assessing needs and designing interventions to meet those needs are skills at the centre of working with at-risk children and their families. However, when it comes to assessing our own needs and interventions to meet those needs as practitioners working in trauma-laden environments, we often fall short. At-risk children and their families need grounded practitioners who can identify what their professional support and professional development needs are. I designed the TISS model to guide practitioners towards creating a more holistic yet pragmatic view of support that acknowledges the deeply complex practice environment.

There are a number of barriers cited in the research literature that reduce a practitioner's ability to seek assistance when they start to experience symptoms of occupational traumatic stress. One of the most common barriers I have already discussed in previous chapters, that is, the fear of being seen as not cut out for the work, dislocating a practitioner from the safety of their professional relationships (Oates, 2019, 2023).

In my own research (Oates, 2019), practitioners voiced their strong reluctance to voice their experiences of occupational traumatic stress for fear of being ridiculed or ostracised, labelled as incompetent, not 'cut out' for child protection work or sanctioned as retribution for speaking out:

> *They might be worried that it could make it worse, they might lose their job. There's a whole range of reasons why they wouldn't talk about it with anybody. You know, they might be just dismissed, like, you know, be told to grow a spine or something. Or just not believed.*
>
> – Lisa

> *There was almost a culture of if you say you're not coping, then you immediately become incompetent and you're immediately treated as being incompetent . . . basically, 'if you guys can't cope, maybe you should work somewhere else'. So it's almost like you don't want to speak up then because people think you can't do your job properly.*
>
> – Mary

> *I guess in some respects it's frowned upon, it's almost like, you know, 'Oh, get over yourself', you know, 'If you want to work in this place, you need to harden up'.*
>
> – Matilda

Practitioners also identified concern that their career prospects, like promotions, may be negatively impacted. Reluctance to disclose the experience of occupational trauma symptoms for fear of being viewed as deficient is reported by practitioners in the research literature (Hunt et al., 2016; Oates, 2019; Zerubavel & Wright, 2012). Pearlman (1995) argued that vicarious traumatisation is not a 'reflection of inadequacy on the part of the [practitioner] . . . it is best conceptualised as an occupational hazard' (p. 52). However, despite Pearlman's (1995) view that the experience of traumatic stress in those who work in trauma-laden environments is inevitable and should be considered an occupational hazard, the literature suggests that child protection agencies struggle to manage the presentation of vicarious trauma and other trauma-based mental health concerns among practitioners (Fink-Samnick, 2022; Goddard & Hunt, 2011; Littlechild, 2005), and that individual workers are often expected to manage their own wellbeing (Lewig & McLean, 2016).

## Practitioners who are line supervisors and managers

In my first book about the TISS model, I included a whole chapter on line supervisors and managers. Often this group of practitioners are overlooked in the research literature regarding what their unique support needs might be and how organisations can more effectively support these needs. The frequency and type of supervision practitioners are entitled to can vary widely between organisations and jurisdictions. For line supervisors and managers, it can be even more varied including seldom receiving formal supervision if at all (Griffiths et al., 2019).

> *I have been a manager in a government agency working with vulnerable children for 12 years. I don't get supervision internally. The time I spend with my line supervisor is about managing problems and putting out fires. It's also about HR issues, staffing and budget management.*
>
> – PJ

In my own research, line supervisors and managers who worked for non-government organisations that delivered services to at-risk children and their families were most likely to be entitled to ongoing external supervision that was funded by their organisation. Line supervisors and managers who had worked in statutory child protection agencies on the whole reported either never receiving supervision or only receiving task-focused supervision. Some reported being able to access external supervision at their own cost. This is consistent with a study by McCrae et al. (2015), which found that supervisors in child welfare organisations did not receive adequate supervision or support. The research literature suggests that line supervisors who received adequate professional support would be more likely to successfully manage the unique dynamics of their role and thus more effectively manage their teams (Collins-Camargo & Antle, 2018; McCrae et al., 2015).

Positional and professional accountability is another unique source of stress for line supervisors and managers that is seldom recognised. Occupational stressors that are unique to line supervisors and managers can include the responsibility 'when things go wrong' including serious non-accidental injury and death of children as well as managing unallocated caseloads due to staff shortages and the risks to children within those cases. Geoffrion et al. (2016) describe stress as a result of positional and professional accountability as an under-researched phenomenon experienced by professionals working within a child welfare context.

> *Early in my career as a case worker I was involved in a child death review. I didn't know the child that died, I just took the intake call. The policy at the time was anyone that had been professionally involved had to be interviewed. It was a harrowing process. I got asked lots of questions about my team leader and manager like what kind of support they offered, how they managed workloads etc – they were asking to see if that was a factor in the child's death. Now I am a manager I think about that interview often – that could easily be one of my workers being interviewed about my performance and how that contributed to a child's death. It weighs on my mind.*
>
> – Teena

Another unique need identified by line managers and supervisors is the lack of formal leadership training for those who progress from frontline practice roles into leadership roles. Regarding the progression of practitioners into leadership positions, the research literature identifies several issues including the lack of leadership and/or management training in undergraduate degrees (Knee & Folsom, 2012; Peters, 2018) and that often practitioners find themselves managing teams for long periods or permanently without sufficient qualifications, skills or experience (Carpenter et al., 2013; Hair, 2013; Kadushin & Harkness, 2014; Wells et al., 2025).

> *My first leadership role was a holiday backfill for four weeks. That manager never came back so I just stayed in the role. That was five years ago. I have never had any management training – I just muddled my way through.*
>
> – Gayle

Additionally, there is a lack of training in relation to how line supervisors and managers can best support the wellbeing needs of practitioners they are responsible for (Berger & Quiros, 2016; Goddard & Hunt, 2011; Jankoski, 2010).

Line supervisors and managers may wish to include professional development in relation to leadership and management as part of their own TISS plan. Mentoring with a more experienced leader or coaching sessions may be appropriate as an additional form of support. They may also want to include professional development in relation to the supervision of practitioners working in trauma-laden environments.

## The wounded healer

The concept of the wounded healer was introduced by Jung in the 1950s to describe those with a personal history of trauma who work in the healing professions. I briefly touched on the wounded healer construct in my first book about the TISS model. The inclusion of the concept related to common ethical dilemmas experienced by line supervisors and managers in the context of supervision. In my own supervision work with practitioners, I have found that acknowledging my own history of trauma and the delicate balance that is required when working with others who have experienced trauma has opened a different level of engagement with supervisees. The disclosure of my own wounded healer identity has provided an opportunity for supervisees to explore their wounded healer identity in the context of their work with children at risk and their families in a professional setting without the fear that disclosure will impact them at work negatively. Safety and empowerment creation within the supervisory relationship is a critical element for practitioners to feel able to deconstruct their own histories of trauma and to safely and critically reflect on the possible connection to emerging occupational trauma symptomology. This is why I have chosen to explore the concept of the wounded healer in this book.

Many practitioners are drawn to the helping professions due to their own history of trauma, hardship and abuse and/or neglect. It is unknown what percentage of the helping professions are staffed by those with their own history of trauma; however, in my experience as a practitioner, supervisor and educator in the field, the number would be significant. There is some consensus in the literature that practitioners who have a history of trauma can possess innate qualities that complement their professional skills and knowledge like increased empathy and ability to work with complexity (Newcomb et al., 2015; Wheeler, 2007; Zerubavel & Wright, 2012). Conversely, there are views cited in the literature that, without appropriate organisational support, practitioners with lived experience of trauma are at risk of being viewed by their organisation in a negative light due to the demonstration of negative wounded healer attributes (Zerubavel & Wright, 2012).

It is my view that the wounded healer has a powerful place in the child and family practice landscape. Harnessing one's own experience combined with professional skills, knowledge and experience places them in a unique position where they may have an increased capacity for empathy, see patterns or signs during assessment that others don't or be able to more effectively build rapport with those being assessed. Anecdotally, wounded healers also possess the capacity to connect with and support other wounded healers in a workplace context. While wounded healers can be extremely influential in an occupational context, it is imperative that they keep well. Keeping well takes maintenance. Deliberate, planned and executed maintenance. Maintaining boundaries is also critical. It could be useful to include support in relation to this in one's individual TISS plan.

## Examining personal practitioner attributes

A key part of the practitioner pillar is to examine what characteristics you possess as a practitioner that may need to be considered when designing your own TISS plan. For example:

| | |
|---|---|
| Are you neurodivergent? | Live with disability? |
| Have a chronic health condition? | Have caring responsibilities at home? |
| Are you in active grief? | Do you have a trauma background that you need additional support in managing? |
| Are you struggling with anxiety, depression or another mental health condition? | Carry a heavy cultural load? |

There has been a tendency in the human and social services to separate one's personal self from one's work self. While it is important to have ethical boundaries when working with at-risk children and their families, it is my view that integrating a practitioner's needs and current circumstances in their TISS plan is a healthy way of ensuring practitioners receive the individualised supports they require to undertake their paid role effectively. I am in no way suggesting that these personal attributes be shared with your line supervisor or manager. Rather, this is an exercise for individual practitioners to consider in their own time, decide what support would be useful and then include that in their TISS plan. For example, the support you arrange could be external supervision. The personal attribute that option provides for the practitioner is the space to unpack how past traumas may be triggered by the work undertaken as part of a practitioner's role. Another example might be that a practitioner starts work early and finishes early. That option might be included in the TISS plan to assist practitioners managing a chronic health condition where fatigue by the end of the day is a feature. Similar to the third central acknowledgement, namely a practitioner's professional support needs will change over time, so will personal attributes that require support.

## Barriers

It is important to examine our own context as practitioners in relation to what our own barriers might be and what a plan might look like to overcome them. Whether your barrier is a lack of trust in the supervisory relationship, a toxic work environment, a fear of being ostracised by peers, concern about promotion, a desire to keep your own experience of trauma private or a combination of these factors, identifying them will assist practitioners to plan to receive support from additional sources so that these barriers can be managed in a healthy, proactive way. Barriers that limit a practitioner's ability to seek support when required are usually a reflection of the organisational culture a practitioner is working in rather than a reflection of the practitioner. However, working through the TISS model can assist practitioners to have more control over their support needs including when and how to seek support when needed rather than being solely reliant on their organisation which as previously explored, is problematic.

## Reflective activity

- What drew you to work with at-risk children and their families? What keeps you in the field?
- Job satisfaction – what gives you job satisfaction? What would increase your feeling of job satisfaction?
- What barriers exist that would stop you from accessing supports? What would address those barriers so that you could seek additional support when needed?
- What elements need to be present to increase your feeling of safety within the supervisory relationship?

- If you are a line supervisor or manager, what additional supports do you need to increase your capacity to undertake your role?
- What are your career progression goals? Where would you like to be in 3–5 years' time? What resources would you need to help you get there?

Notes:

## The supervisor (and the TISS team)

The supervisor pillar relates not only to a practitioner's line supervisor, but also to the other people involved in supporting an individual's TISS plan. That may include other senior professionals in a practitioner's workplace, an external supervisor, peers involved in a peer support capacity or a cultural mentor, as examples.

**The line supervisor or manager**: Firstly, I will explore the supervisory relationship between a practitioner and their line supervisor or manager. A strong and robust supervisory relationship has been cited in the research literature to contribute to a practitioners ability to critically explore and improve their practice (Little et al., 2018; Radey & Stanley, 2018), increase feelings of psychological safety (Kruzich et al., 2014), increase job satisfaction (Hunt et al., 2016; Regehr, 2018), and build healthy professional resiliency (Beddoe et al., 2014; McFadden, 2020; Regehr, 2018). Further, authors in the research literature have identified the supervisory relationship as a key factor in practitioner wellbeing and a protective measure in relation to the experience of occupational traumatic stress symptomology (Berger & Quiros, 2016; Davys & Beddoe, 2010; McPherson et al., 2016; Oates, 2023; Pack, 2015). The ability of supervisors to facilitate a practitioner's sharing of emotional distress and to safely lead them to a place where critical reflection and eventually integrated learning can occur is critical to the professional development of the practitioner as well as a strategy to safeguard against internalising occupational traumatic stress.

Exploring threats to the supervisory relationship, given the clear evidence that supervisory relationships are critical to practitioner wellbeing is a feature of the TISS model. Uncomfortable feelings can arise from supervision for the practitioner, even when being challenged respectfully, to reflect on things that might not have gone so well. This is a healthy part of the supervision process and to a practitioner's ongoing professional development. Managing these uncomfortable feelings in an upfront, professionally mature way can mitigate threats to the overall supervisory relationship. Key threats to a successful supervisory relationship identified in the research literature include a lack of consistency, a perceived lack of commitment of the supervisor to the wellbeing of the practitioner being supervised, and practitioner perception that supervision is a surveillance tool for performance management. It must be noted that although these three elements are repeatedly listed in the research literature, a useful endeavour would be for supervisors and practitioners to identify what they feel might pose a threat to the supervisory relationship and strategies they feel might mitigate those risks.

Achieving the mitigation of risks within a practitioner's TISS plan can be planned for in several ways. To begin with, the power of acknowledgement cannot be underestimated. Acknowledging that there will be times when the supervisory relationship is strained and planning for those times is a useful strategy. Examples might include exploring how a practitioner might let their line supervisor know that they need some time to process uncomfortable feelings that emerge from supervision. Another example might be exploring what actions or behaviours a line supervisor or manager would have to demonstrate for a practitioner to feel that they are committed to their professional development and wellbeing. These clear, professionally mature conversations in supervision are critical, particularly when a common symptom of occupational traumatic stress can be the inability to interpret interactions with others accurately.

While the research literature is clear regarding the importance of the supervisory relationship in the context of practitioner wellbeing, line supervisors and managers attract a reasonable amount of criticism in the research literature about their inability to provide effective supervision to staff. Key reasons for this are identified in the literature include organisational constraints like resourcing, internal organisational culture and negative perceptions held by practitioners about the purpose of supervision (Beddoe & Davys, 2016; Hunt et al., 2016; Oates, 2019, 2023). However, it must be noted that while this is the experience of participants in those studies, it doesn't always tell the whole story. As mentioned previously, single practitioners are but a tiny cog in a large complex system. The same is true for individual line supervisors and managers.

Child protection systems are risk-averse by nature. Risk-adverse organisational cultures can reduce the capacity of line supervisors to provide supervision to practitioners internally as organisational and political priorities take primary importance (Oates, 2023). While the goal of any line supervisor or manager is to ensure that quality evidence-based services are delivered to clients and practitioners, an organisation's focus on organisational and political imperatives is internally driven, often by executive administrators, and therefore often beyond the control of individual supervisors and line managers.

Reflecting on one of the central acknowledgements that underpin the TISS model, namely, that a practitioner's professional development and wellbeing support cannot be solely managed by their line supervisor or manager, it is my view that a re-assessment of the role the line supervisor or manager plays within the broader context of a practitioner's support and supervision plan is required as already discussed in previous chapters. There is support in the research literature to reassess the role of the line supervisor (Oates, 2023; Perry et al., 2020; Rankine, 2018). Additionally, it must be acknowledged that re-assessing the role of the line supervisor or manager has benefits for the line supervisor or manager as well. The onerous workloads of line supervisors and managers are a barrier to providing for all the support and professional development needs of the practitioners they supervise. Further, line supervisors and managers often don't have the delegation required to increase the level of resourcing needed to adequately meet the needs of staff. Dispersing the responsibility of providing support to practitioners (including to the practitioners themselves) will not only increase the possibility that practitioners will receive the support they require, but it also eases the burden of constantly failing to provide adequate supervision to staff. The TISS model acknowledges this and normalises that practitioners need multiple sources of support to effectively have their needs met.

## Other members of the TISS team

**External supervisor:** A key source of external support relied on by a number of practitioners is the provision of external supervision. External supervision is usually provided by an experienced private practitioner, not employed by the practitioner's organisation, on a fee-for-service basis. Funding arrangements for external supervision vary and can include sessions funded entirely by a practitioner's organisation, partly funded by a practitioner's organisation (the difference to be funded by the practitioner) or solely funded by the practitioner themselves. Most organisations have a policy that practitioners can access external supervision sessions during paid work time; however, that can vary between organisations. Some practitioners will seek an external supervisor who shares the same professional background as them, like social work, psychology or nursing as examples. This could be to satisfy professional association requirements in addition to the other benefits afforded to practitioners who undertake external supervision.

Participants in my doctoral research shared their thoughts on engaging in professional supervision while working with at-risk children and their families:

> *You're able to go and get things off your chest. The weight off your shoulder. For your own mental wellbeing, because what we take on every day is huge. To be able to talk to people and get stuff off your chest on hard cases is important*
>
> – Missy

> *I think that outside supervision is good just to have that, you know, if stuff's building up and you're not able to talk to anybody, then you've got somebody that you can actually go out and talk to and it's somebody that you've chosen yourself.*
>
> – Lisa

Additionally, many practitioners who participated in my doctoral research stated that external supervision described it as an opportunity to discuss personal and professional matters without fear. Participants used words such as 'freedom', 'safe' and 'private' to describe their experiences with external supervision. The participants expressed a reluctance to express their needs fully during internal supervision, primarily because of fear of being judged unfairly by their supervisor or being viewed as incompetent:

> *You risk judgement being passed from a supervisor. So it's more about just sharing what you need to share within a work framework. Whereas the external one is unload without the fear of 'my boss is going to take this and do something with it', or 'and it's going to go on my file'. It is somewhere safe to go.*
>
> – David

> *It just gave me the freedom, I suppose, to feel like, okay, whoever I'm talking to, it's definitely not – there's no connection to [participant's workplace] in any way.*
>
> – Alice

> *I can tell [external supervisor] anything and everything and she listens and advises me. But yeah, she doesn't have that connection back here. Because I feel you just don't – when you work in a place where you're not fully trusting of everyone within that organisation, it can be a concern if you want to go yarn to someone about something. So the fact that you can go and talk to someone totally outside of [participant's workplace] is good. Very good.*
>
> – Missy

In my own research, external supervision was found to be universally welcomed by practitioners working with at-risk children and their families due to the private and safe space it affords them to unpack issues pertaining to their work as well as their wellbeing.

**Peer support**: As outlined in previous chapters, the inclusion of peer support in a practitioner's TISS plan is recommended. There is comfort in conversing with other professionals who understand the type of work practitioners working with at-risk children and their families undertake as well as the environment in which they undertake that work in. As mentioned previously, engaging in peer support with other practitioners in this field gives the opportunity to have frank and open conversations about the work and the environment in which work is undertaken. This sense of community can be very therapeutic, especially in relation to managing occupational traumatic stress.

However, as mentioned in previous chapters, not all peer support is 'safe'. While there are expectations that what is discussed remains confidential, it is not the same as the privacy one is afforded in a formal external supervision arrangement. It could be useful while planning to consider what you are prepared to share in these sessions and what would be best left for an external supervision type arrangement. While engaging in peer support is completely up to the individual practitioner, it would be my recommendation, as previously mentioned, to have at least some semi-formal structure and that it be formally written into a practitioner's TISS plan.

**Cultural, religious, or spiritual mentor**: Some practitioners may choose to include a cultural, religious or spiritual advisor in their TISS plans. This could be done by way of choosing an external supervisor with those attributes or it could look like the inclusion of attendance at certain events or meetings with individuals on a regular basis. As mentioned, TISS plans have the practitioner at the centre. While the inclusion of a cultural, religious or spiritual mentor is completely up to the practitioner, if this element is to be included, I would recommend that a semi-structured format be included as a minimum to give it legitimacy so that these sessions can be undertaken in work time.

## Reflective activity

- What would you need to achieve a strong supervisory relationship with your line supervisor or manager? What would that look like day to day?
- Thinking back on the chapter where I detailed the trauma informed principles in the context of the TISS model – what do you need to achieve safety within your support and supervision arrangements?
- Do you need supervision from someone who shares your professional qualifications? For example, an accredited social work or psychology supervisor
- What would you like to seek outside supervision for? What are you prepared to share with your line supervisor about yourself and your personal circumstances?
- If you feel your current line supervisor is not providing you with the elements of support that you require, where could you source additional support from?

Notes:

____________________________________________________________

____________________________________________________________

## The organisation

The organisation pillar refers to the organisation practitioner's work for. It is established in the research literature that organisations, across jurisdictions, struggle to provide the practitioners who deliver services to at-risk children and their families adequate supervision (Beddoe & Davys, 2016; Hunt et al., 2016; McCrae et al., 2015; Oates, 2019, 2023, Wells et al., 2025). It must be noted that I don't think organisations intentionally fail their practitioners in this way. I acknowledge that the lack of support to practitioners is a systems failure that is complex in origin, and if it were easy to alter, it would have been before now. Child welfare systems reviews have been recommended in several studies (Hunt et al., 2016; Littlechild, 2005; Munro, 2010; Oates, 2019) so that the systemic and cultural deficits that create the lack of support afforded to practitioners can be identified and addressed.

In my first book about the TISS model, I included a whole chapter on line supervisors and managers, which included a critique of managerialism and how it impacts organisational ability to effectively support practitioners who work with at-risk children and their families. I will include some of that work in this chapter. Authors like Beddoe and Davys (2016) and Hughes and Wearing (2017) acknowledge that the roles taken on by human services professionals, including their practice, are often defined or prescribed by the employing organisation. Exploring organisational impacts on practice is therefore necessary. Additionally, if practitioners are aware of how organisations operate including how organisational cultures form, they are much better placed to see themselves as part of a system rather than an individual practitioner with deficits that need correction.

The rise of managerialism has had one of the greatest impacts on the human and social service delivery landscape in the past few decades. Neoliberalism is the ideological position that underpins managerialism. The tenets of neoliberalism heavily rely on the principles of the market to inform operational policy and practice (Ferguson & Lavalette, 2013). Key services once delivered by government being outsourced, reliance on short-term contracts, and/or labour hire agencies are examples, as are organisational restructures, rebranding and continuous efficiency reviews (Carey, 2015).

The research literature identifies managerialism as a barrier to the provision of quality supervision to practitioners in the workplace (Hughes & Wearing, 2017; Noble & Irwin, 2009). The neoliberal ideology views organisations as the deliverers of services. However, absent within the ideology is organisational responsibility to develop, nurture and appropriately support the practitioners who deliver those services to at-risk children and their families. Many jurisdictions are facing ongoing austerity measures, meaning if a practitioner is not receiving the support internally within their organisation that they require, the onus is on them to source alternative supports and cover the costs themselves:

> *I have been a line manager in a child welfare agency for 8 years. Over that time the workload has increased exponentially. Staff are leaving the sector in greater numbers than I have seen before. All the cases with no case worker rest with me. There is no money in the budget for additional help. I constantly cancel supervision because of one crisis or another. I tell staff to get external supervision because at least*

*that way they will get support. They have to pay for it themselves as well as there is no budget for it internally.*

– Georgia

The research literature also notes that managerialist organisational cultures negatively impact the quality of supervision provided to practitioners. Noble and Irwin (2009) cite that managerialist organisational climates tend towards the provision of supervision that is compliance-driven rather than centred around practitioner need. This is inconsistent with evidence-based best practice, which outlines that compliance-driven models of supervision which are heavily administrative do not sufficiently meet the needs of practitioners working with at-risk children and their families (Beddoe et al., 2021; Bradbury-Jones, 2013; Ferguson, 2011; Goddard & Hunt, 2011; Manthorpe et al., 2015; Wilkins et al., 2017).

Organisational environments that view practitioners as resources (an operational cost that efficiency measures can be applied to, replaceable) instead of assets (whose knowledge and expertise increase the capacity of the organisation to deliver quality core services), reduce the capacity of practitioners to use their expertise to inform systemic change. In a social service delivery context, top-down managerialist-driven organisations have been shown to be problematic as practitioners are not units of stock and vulnerable children and families are not liabilities to efficiency (Hughes & Wearing, 2017). Evidence-based practice and ongoing evaluation should drive innovation and change, not market forces which are central to neoliberal and managerialist ideology (Ferguson & Lavalette, 2013).

Given the above, what is a practitioner to do if the organisation they are working for does not support the provision of quality supervision to staff? It is my firm unwavering belief that organisations should provide their practitioners with individualised support and supervision that is responsive to need. However, I am also not naïve to the fact that organisations, particularly those delivering services to at-risk children and their families, struggle to provide quality supervision to their practitioners. They also struggle with other complexities including toxic work environments, onerous media scrutiny, unmanageable workloads, legislative, political and resource constraints as well as persistent staff turnover (Radey & Wilke, 2023; Hunt et al., 2016; Oates, 2019; Wells et al., 2025).

Having practitioners understand their location within a larger system can assist them in working through feelings of occupational traumatic stress. An example of this might be when practitioners develop a sense of hopelessness working within the 'system'. In my time working with practitioners, it is almost always the 'system' that contributes to a practitioner's decision to leave their role, rather than the work with at-risk children and their families. Internalised hopelessness and the feeling that the work practitioners do is meaningless can be overwhelming. This paralysis can lead to practitioners not fully engaging in their work or monitoring their own wellbeing. Supporting practitioners to externalise their feelings of hopelessness is an effective strategy for practitioners to undertake as it might assist them to move through uncomfortable feelings that can arise as a result of working in this area.

The TISS model seeks to acknowledge the inherent complexities, including structural and political, that come with working with at-risk children and their families. Identifying these complexities assists with the development of mitigation strategies that can be included within a practitioner's TISS plan. An example of this might be acknowledging organisational complexities pertaining to practitioner workloads. In most jurisdictions and practice settings, there are policy and procedural guides outlining expectations in relation to workload, especially when it comes to the number of cases an individual practitioner may have responsibility for. However, anyone who has worked in a child welfare organisation knows that there can be a chasm between ideal workloads and reality. Child welfare organisations are plagued by high staff turnover rates and difficulty recruiting and retaining experienced practitioners, especially in rural and remote communities. Mitigation strategies to be included in a practitioner's TISS plan might include workload as a standing agenda item. This will open the opportunity for frank dialogue between a practitioner and their line supervisor or manager regarding questions like what the timeframe might be for when a practitioner's excessive workload might be reduced, how unmet targets might be managed, and additional requirements for support, like administrative support during the time period, for example. The power of acknowledging that unreasonable workloads are the product of a system's failure rather than the failings of an individual practitioner cannot be underestimated. Having workload, in the context that we are speaking about, as a standing agenda item within a practitioner's TISS plan will give the practitioner a sense of safety to raise these issues without the fear of being deemed as not suitable for the position if they cannot keep up with the workload.

## Reflective activity

- What is the organisational culture within the organisation you work for?
- What are the constraints within your organisation? For example, resourcing, staff churn, workloads, and overworked leadership?
- How could you include strategies in your TISS plan regarding unreasonable workloads?

- How do these constraints impact your support and supervision arrangements? If negatively, what outside supports can be sourced?

Notes:

## Local contextualisation

The fourth pillar underpinning the TISS model is local contextualisation. The local contextualisation pillar guides practitioners to consider how their local context impacts their work and their wellbeing. The local context in which practitioners are working has a direct impact on wellbeing; however, it is seldom included in traditional supervision models. For example, the smaller the community a practitioner works in, the more visible they become. Practitioners working in regional towns will regularly interact with the at-risk children and families they work with during the day in their nonwork life. These interactions may occur through shared children's activities, attendance at the same church or sporting groups:

> *I worked in a regional community when my kids were little. There was only one primary school. The best friend of one of my kids was a child in foster care. That child's foster carer and I would always be in each other's orbit – school events, sports carnivals etc. My office was responsible for renewing fostering accreditations as well as investigating concerns raised in foster placements. Nothing ever happened but I often wondered, what would happen if my child's friend's placement had to be investigated? What would that mean for my child and their friendship?*
>
> – Leesa

Working with at-risk children and their families, as previously outlined, brings with it some occupational inevitabilities including working with angry parents. Increased visibility when living and working in the same community can negatively impact practitioner wellbeing including altering how they conduct themselves outside of the office:

> *In the town I work in there are only two supermarkets. I would shop at obscure times to minimise the chance of running into parents I have removed children from. I mean I would be angry too. But after working all day the last thing I want is to manage an uncomfortable interaction in a public space like a supermarket. I would just get in and out as soon as I could – there was increased anxiety for sure, always feeling on guard.*
>
> – Jaye

> *Try dating in the regional town you do child protection work in – you never know who is connected to who. It's impossible.*
>
> – Irene

The inability to get distance between one's work life and one's home life can erode a practitioner's sense of internal safety, never really getting a break. Also, the feeling of being restricted in how you spend time and who you spend time with can be extremely difficult.

Working in communities where visibility is increased can also impact the comfort of practitioners accessing other professionals:

> *I started a new role in a town of about 5000 people. I needed to see a doctor when I arrived to get prescriptions renewed for my antidepressant medication and contraception method. Because I was a new patient the doctor had to take a detailed medical history – physical health, mental health, family life everything. The following week I was sitting in a case conference with the same doctor – I was mortified.*
>
> – Shea

> *I had to see a psychologist in a neighbouring town – I couldn't see the same psychologist as all the kids on my case load, that wouldn't feel right.*
>
> – Anika

Acknowledging and planning for these complexities within the context of the TISS model can give back a sense of control and ownership to the practitioner. Things one might include in a TISS plan could be the exploration of seeking professionals outside of the community with access via phone or video appointments. As previously mentioned, the power of acknowledging these additional pressures cannot be underestimated. Openly naming and discussing these challenges can be extremely beneficial.

In relation to the physical community that practitioners work in, gaining a solid understanding of the sociological, economic and political factors that impact life in that community is invaluable information for practitioners to have. Understanding these elements and being able to analyse community issues from this framework is a strategy that will facilitate a practitioner's ability to externalise some of the occupational traumatic stress they may experience.

Questions that a practitioner and their supports may ask themselves within a local contextualisation context might include:

- What is the history of the community we work in? Does the community have a history of traumatic events like ongoing military conflict, natural disasters, dispossession of land due to colonisation or high rates of humanitarian settlement?
- What is the demographic landscape of the community? Does the community have a lot of older people in comparison to younger people and families as an example? Are there large numbers of migrant or newly arrived people who don't have English as a first language?

- What socioeconomic factors impact the community? Is the community deemed to be predominantly lower socioeconomic in categorisation? What are the unemployment rates? Is there adequate access to housing, education, healthcare and other social support services? Is there an above average incarceration rate?

As previously mentioned, many of the factors outlined in this core pillar are excluded from traditional supervision models. However, considering them in a structured framework such as the TISS model can be extremely beneficial for practitioners as these factors can have enormous impacts on practitioner wellbeing and their overall capacity to work effectively with at-risk children and their families.

## Reflective activity

- What is the local context of the community you work in?
- Are there any specific factors that would impact your wellbeing? Your ability to undertake the work?
- Are there any concerns or worries you have about working in your community?
- Do you have appropriate access to the professionals you need to support your own professional development and wellbeing? If not, what mitigation strategies would you include in your own TISS plan?

Notes:

## Chapter summary

In this chapter the four central pillars that support the TISS model were discussed, namely, the practitioner; the supervisor (and TISS team); the organisation; and local contextualisation. The reflective activities included are to provide practitioners the opportunity to engage with the material in preparation for the development of their own TISS plan. Examining individual needs through a framework like this will assist practitioners to identify what their actual needs might be. Once identified, mitigation strategies can be designed and implemented to more effectively support the individual needs of practitioners.

## References

Beddoe, L., & Davys, A. (2016). *Challenges in professional supervision: Current themes and models for practice*. London: Jessica Kingsley Publishers.

Beddoe, L., Davys, A., & Adamson, C. (2014). "Never trust anybody who says 'I don't need supervision'": Practitioners beliefs about social worker resilience. *Practice (Birmingham, England)*, *26*(2), 113–130. https://doi.org/10.1080/09503153.2014.896888

Beddoe, L., Ferguson, H., Warwick, L., Disney, T., Leigh, J., & Cooner, T. S. (2021). Supervision in child protection: A space and place for reflection or an excruciating marathon of compliance? *European*

*Journal of Social Work*, *25*(3), 525–537. https://doi.org/10.1080/13691457.2021.1964443

Berger, R., & Quiros, L. (2016). Best practices for training trauma-informed practitioners: Supervisors' voice. *Traumatology*, *22*(2), 145–154. https://doi.org/10.1037/trm0000076

Bradbury-Jones, C. (2013). Refocusing child protection supervision: An innovative approach to supporting practitioners. *Child Care in Practice*, *19*(3), 253–266. https://doi.org/10.1080/13575279.2013.785937

Carey, M. (2015). The fragmentation of social work and social care: Some ramifications and a critique. *British Journal of Social Work*, *45*(8), 2406–2422. https://doi.org/10.1093/bjsw/bcu088

Carpenter, J., Webb, C., & Bostock, L. (2013). The surprisingly weak evidence base for supervision: Findings from a systematic review of research in child welfare practice (2000–2012). *Children and Youth Services Review*, *35*(11), 1843–1853. https://doi.org/10.1016/j.childyouth.2013.08.014

Collins-Camargo, C., & Antle, B. (2018). Child welfare supervision: Special issues related to trauma-informed care in a unique environment. *The Clinical Supervisor*, *37*(1), 64–82. https://doi.org/10.1080/07325223.2017.1382412

Davys, A., & Beddoe, L. (2010). *Best practice in professional supervision: A guide for the helping professions*. London, England: Jessica Kingsley.

Ferguson, H. (2011). *Child protection practice*. Basingstoke, England: Palgrave MacMillan.

Ferguson, I., & Lavalette, M. (2013). Crisis, austerity and the future(s) of social work in the UK. *Critical and Radical Social Work*, *1*(1), 95–110. https://doi.org/10.1332/204986013X665992

Fink-Samnick, E. (2022). Collective occupational trauma, health care quality, and trauma-informed leadership: Intersections and implications. *Professional Case Management*, *27*(3), 107–123. https://doi.org/10.1097/NCM.0000000000000559

Geoffrion, S., Morselli, C., & Guay, S. (2015/2016). Rethinking compassion fatigue through the lens of professional identity: The case of child-protection workers. *Trauma, Violence & Abuse*, *17*(3), 270–283. https://doi.org/10.1177/1524838015584362

Goddard, C., & Hunt, S. (2011). The complexities of caring for child protection workers: The contexts of practice and supervision. *Journal of Social Work Practice*, *25*(4), 413–432. https://doi.org/0.1080/02650533.2011.626644

Griffiths, A., Desrosiers, P., Gabbard, J., Royse, D., & Piescher, K. (2019). Retention of child welfare caseworkers: The wisdom of supervisors. *Child Welfare*, *97*(3), 61–84. https://www.jstor.org/stable/48623658

Hair, H. (2013). The purpose and duration of supervision, and the training and discipline of supervisors: What social workers say they need to provide effective services. *The British Journal of Social Work*, *43*, 1562–1588. http://dx.doi.org/10.1093/ bjsw/bcs071

Hughes, M., & Wearing, M. (2017). *Organisations and management in social work: Everyday action for change* (3rd ed.). London: SAGE Publications.

Hunt, S., Goddard, C., Cooper, J., Littlechild, B., & Wild, J. (2016). "If I feel like this, how does the child feel?" Child protection workers, supervision, management and organisational responses to parental violence. *Journal of Social Work Practice*, *30*(1), 5–24. https://doi.org/10.1080/02650533.2015.1073145

Jankoski, J. (2010). Is vicarious trauma the culprit? A study of child welfare professionals. *Child Welfare*, *89*(6), 105–131.

Kadushin, A., & Harkness, D. (2014). *Supervision in social work* (5th ed.). Columbia University Press.

Knee, R., & Folsom, J. (2012). Bridging the crevasse between direct practice social work and management by increasing the transferability of core skills. *Administration in Social Work*, *36*, 390–408. https://doi.org/10.1080/03643107.2011.604402

Kruzich, J., Mienko, J., & Courtney, M. (2014). Individual and work group influences on turnover intention among public child welfare workers: The effects of work group psychological safety. *Children and Youth Services Review*, *42*, 20–27. https://doi.org/10.1016/j.childyouth.2014.03.005

Lewig, K., & McLean, S. (2016). *Caring for our frontline child protection workforce (CFCA paper no. 42)*. Melbourne, VIC: Child Family Community Australia Information Exchange, Australian Institute of Family Studies.

Little, M., Baker, T., & Jinks, A. (2018). A qualitative evaluation of community nurses' experiences of child safeguarding supervision. *Child Abuse Review*, *27*(2), 150–157. http://dx.doi.org/10.1002/car.2493

Littlechild, B. (2005). The nature and effects of violence against child-protection social workers: Providing effective support. *The British Journal of Social Work*, *35*(3), 387–401. https://doi.org/10.1093/bjsw/bch188

Manthorpe, J., Moriarty, J., Hussein, S., Stevens, M., & Sharpe, E. (2015). Content and purpose of supervision in social work practice in England: Views of newly qualified social workers, managers and directors. *British Journal of Social Work*, *45*(1), 52–68. https://doi.org/10.1093/bjsw/bct102

McCrae, J., Scannapieco, M., & Obermann, A. (2015). Retention and job satisfaction of child welfare supervisors. *Children and Youth Services Review*, *59*, 171–176. https://doi.org/10.1016/j.childyouth.2015.11.011

McFadden, P. (2020). Two sides of one coin? Relationships build resilience or contribute to burnout in child protection social work: Shared perspectives from leavers and stayers in Northern Ireland. *International Social Work*, *63*(2), 164–176. https://doi.org/10.1177/0020872818788393

McPherson, L., Frederico, M., & McNamara, P. (2016). Safety as a fifth dimension in supervision: Stories from the frontline. *Australian Social Work*, *69*(1), 67–79. https://doi.org/10.1080/0312407X.2015.1024265

Munro, E. (2010). *The Munro review of child protection: Interim report – the child's journey*. London, England: Department of Education.

Newcomb, M., Burton, J., Edwards, N., & Hazelwood, Z. (2015). How Jung's concept of the wounded healer can guide learning and teaching in social work and human services. *Advances in Social Work and Welfare Education*, *17*(2), 55–69.

Noble, C., & Irwin, J. (2009). Social work supervision: An exploration of the current challenges in a rapidly changing social, economic and political environment. *Journal of Social Work*, *9*(3), 345–358. https://doi.org/10.1177/1468017309334848

Oates, F. (2019). You are not allowed to tell: Organisational culture as a barrier for child protection workers seeking assistance for traumatic stress symptomology. *Children Australia*, *44*(2), 84–90. https://doi.org/10.1017/cha.2019.12

Oates, F. (2023). *Trauma informed support and supervision for child protection professionals: A model for those working with children who have experienced trauma, abuse and neglect and their families* (1st ed.). Routledge. https://doi.org/10.4324/9781003026006

Pack, M. (2015). "Unsticking the stuckness": A qualitative study of the clinical supervisory needs of early-career health social workers. *British Journal of Social Work*, *45*(6), 1821–1836. https://doi.org/10.1093/bjsw/bcu069

Pearlman, L. (1995). Self-care for trauma therapists: Ameliorating vicarious traumatization. In B. Stamm & A. Hudnall (Eds.), *Secondary traumatic stress: Self-care issues for clinicians, researchers, and educators* (pp. 51–64). Baltimore, MD: The Sidran Press.

Perry, M. A., Creavey, K., Arthur, E., Chance Humer, J., Lundgren, P. J., & Rivera, I. (2020). Cultivating emotional intelligence in child welfare professionals: A systematic scoping review. *Child Abuse & Neglect*, *110*(3). https://doi.org/10.1016/j.chiabu.2020.104438

Peters, S. (2018). Defining social work leadership: A theoretical and conceptual review and analysis. *Journal of Social Work Practice*, *32*(1), 31–44. https://doi.org/10.1080/02650533.2017.1300877

Radey, M., & Stanley, L. (2018). "Hands on" versus "empty": Supervision experiences of frontline child welfare workers. *Children and Youth Services Review*, *91*, 128–136. https://doi.org/10.1016/j.childyouth.2018.05.037

Radey, M., & Wilke, D. J. (2023). The importance of job demands and supports: Promoting retention among child welfare workers. *Child & Adolescent Social Work Journal*, *40*(1), 57–69. https://doi.org/10.1007/s10560-021-00762-z

Rankine, M. (2018). How critical are we? Revitalizing critical reflection in supervision. *Advances in Social Work and Welfare Education*, *20*(2), 31–46. https://journal.anzswwer.org/index.php/advances/article/view/133

Regehr, C. (2018). *Stress, trauma, and decision-making for social workers*. New York: Columbia University Press.

Wells, M., Jonsson, L., Keefe, M., & Oates, F. (2025). Supervision and organizational resilience: Considerations for staff retention in child welfare agencies. *International Journal of Child and Adolescent Resilience*, *11*(1), 25–37. https://doi.org/10.54488/ijcar.2024.357

Wheeler, S. (2007). What shall we do with the wounded healer? The supervisor's dilemma. *Psychodynamic Practice*, *13*(3), 245–256. https://doi.org/10.1080/14753630701455838

Wilkins, D., Forrester, D., & Grant, L. (2017). What happens in child and family social work supervision? *Child & Family Social Work*, *22*(2), 942–951. https://doi.org/10.1111/cfs.12314

Zerubavel, N., & Wright, M. (2012). The dilemma of the wounded healer. *Psychotherapy*, *49*(4), 482–491. https://doi.org/10.1037/a0027824

# Part four Creating and implementing a TISS plan

## Introduction

As discussed throughout the book, the TISS model is a scaffolded support and supervision model designed to respond to the individual development and wellbeing needs of practitioners working in trauma-laden environments with at-risk children and their families. Working with at-risk children and their families is one of the most complex areas of human services practice for a variety of reasons. The work is complex. The environment that the work occurs is equally as complex. The workloads are onerous. Negative media coverage is at times relentless. Professionals in adjacent sectors are highly critical. The occupational environments that practitioners work with at-risk children and their families are trauma-laden in nature, with the threat of violence ever present. The lack of outwardly facing trauma responses to extreme situations is often celebrated as practitioner resilience. The TISS model seeks to support practitioners who work with at-risk children and their families, manage their exposure to occupational traumatic stress, so that they are best placed to ensure children are safe and families are supported to increase their capacity to provide for the care and protection needs of their children.

While practitioners are preparing to design their own TISS plan, revisiting the central elements of the TISS model will be useful so they are at the forefront when planning. Those elements being the central acknowledgements, namely, the experience of occupational trauma is an occupational inevitability; a practitioner's professional development and wellbeing support cannot be solely managed by their line supervisor or manager; and a practitioner's professional support needs will change over time; the six trauma informed principles, namely, safety; trustworthiness and transparency; peer support, collaboration and mutuality; empowerment, voice and choice; and cultural, historical and gender considerations; and the four core pillars, namely, the practitioner, the supervisor (and TISS team), the organisation and local contextualisation.

DOI: 10.4324/9781003515371-5

## Revisiting the central acknowledgements underpinning the TISS model

I will now revisit the three central acknowledgements that underpin the TISS model. The three central acknowledgements are:

- the experience of occupational trauma is an occupational inevitability
- a practitioner's professional development and wellbeing support cannot be solely managed by their line supervisor or manager
- a practitioner's professional support needs will change over time

It is important to remember that these three central acknowledgements underpin the TISS model, as there is evidence-based support for their inclusion. The evidence base has been outlined in previous chapters. I will now summarise the three central acknowledgements including the evidence base that supports their inclusion.

The **first acknowledgement**, the experience of occupational traumatic stress is an occupational inevitability, is the genesis of the TISS model. Working with at-risk children and their families is trauma-laden in nature; therefore, it would be impossible for practitioners not to be impacted in some way by the work and the environment in which the work occurs. That being said, organisations still struggle to provide effective support and supervision to practitioners or to manage the onset of problematic occupational traumatic stress symptomologies adequately. As previously outlined, there are a number of barriers identified in the research literature that prevent practitioners from seeking assistance when they start to experience symptoms of occupational traumatic stress. These barriers include a poor supervisory relationship, inadequate resourcing, organisational culture and practitioner perception (Beddoe & Davys, 2016; Hunt et al., 2016; Kruzich et al., 2014; Little et al., 2018; McCrae et al., 2015; Oates, 2019; Radey & Stanley, 2018). It is my position that if organisations had this central acknowledgement as the basis of their operational model, support pathways pre- and post-exposure would be clearer and more effective for practitioners. I acknowledge that organisational change takes time. In the meantime, practitioners can start to address some of these organisational shortfalls by designing and implementing their own TISS plan.

The **second central acknowledgement** is that a practitioner's professional development and wellbeing support cannot be solely managed by their line supervisor or manager. The research literature is clear that the supervisory relationship is critical to practitioners feeling supported in their work (Beddoe et al., 2014; Kruzich et al., 2014; Little et al., 2018; McFadden, 2020; Radey & Stanley, 2018; Regehr, 2018). There are many reasons cited in the research literature that help explain why line supervisors and managers struggle to deliver quality supervision to the practitioners they have line management responsibility for which have been outlined previously. Therefore, there is a strong evidence-based rationale to diversify the sources of support available to practitioners and to rethink the role of the line supervisor or manager as the sole point of support.

The **third central acknowledgement** is that a practitioner's professional support needs will change over time. Anecdotally, once a practitioner's support or development plan is drafted, it is rarely revisited, missing crucial opportunities to assess if the plan meets the current needs of the individual practitioner. These missing opportunities could lead to a reduction in the feeling of job satisfaction experienced by practitioners. The feeling of job satisfaction is crucial as it has been identified in the research literature as being a critical element contributing to the retention of experienced staff in organisations that deliver services to at-risk children and their families (Beddoe et al., 2014; Berger & Quiros, 2016; Hunt et al., 2016; Regehr, 2018). A practitioner's support and professional development needs are fluid and will ebb and flow over time as they become more experienced in their roles. Practitioners feeling stagnant in their professional development may feel compelled to look elsewhere if they are not supported in their roles to grow and to seek additional opportunities to support this growth. TISS plans need to be flexible and have the ability to be responsive to changing practitioner needs. Acknowledging with practitioners that there is an expectation that their needs will change over time facilitates an environment where practitioners have the safety to discuss what their current needs are as well as what their future needs might be.

## Revisiting the six trauma-informed principles in the context of the TISS model

As outlined throughout previous chapters, the TISS model is informed by the six trauma-informed principles, namely, safety; trustworthiness and transparency; peer support, collaboration and mutuality; empowerment, voice and choice; and cultural, historical and gender considerations (SAMHSA, 2014). I have summarised the six trauma-informed principles and how they apply in the context of preparation for designing one's own TISS plan in previous chapters. I will summarise them again here so they are at the forefront of one's mind when going into additional reflective activities throughout this chapter.

The first principle, **safety**, in many ways is the most critical in the context of supervision and support. A lack of safety in the supervisory relationship is repeatedly cited in the research literature as barrier for effective practitioner engagement in the supervision process (Kruzich et al.,

2014; Little et al., 2018; Radey & Stanley, 2018). A lack of safety in supervision can also inform a practitioner's decision not to disclose matters that might be impacting their wellbeing in the workplace including symptoms of occupational traumatic stress (Beddoe et al., 2014; McFadden, 2020; Regehr, 2018). While preparing to design one's own TISS plan, it is important to keep in the fore, what strategies can be implemented to achieve safety in the supervisory relationship. Alternatively, to identify early on that safety may not be able to be achieved in the supervisory relationship for whatever reason and to include mitigation strategies.

The second principle, **trustworthiness and transparency**, in the context of the TISS model, relates to transparency in the supervisory relationship including what the purpose of supervision is and what the sessions might be used for. Several participants in my own research indicated that at times they were suspicious about what supervision was and believed that the sessions were used by their line supervisors as a strategy to performance manage them out of their positions (Oates, 2019). The building and maintenance of trust in the supervisory relationship are critical and have been identified in the research literature as a key factor in a practitioner's ability to move through traumatic occupational experiences. As mentioned earlier, it is equally important to identify where trust and transparency may not be able to be achieved and to include mitigation strategies.

The third principle, **peer support**, in the context of the TISS model refers to the support a practitioner receives from their peers in either a formal or informal capacity. Usually, peer support comes from those who are colleagues, not involved in the practitioner's line supervision. In my own research, several participants felt a greater sense of safety to share exactly what they have been experiencing with someone (peer or supervisor) who has also worked with children at risk and their families, feeling that unless you have done this kind of work, you can never fully understand what it is like and therefore the impacts. Peer support can be an extremely valuable addition to a practitioner's TISS plan. However, peer support should not be the only source of support, as explored in previous chapters.

The fourth principle, **collaboration and mutuality**, in the context of the TISS model, relates to the partnership element of supervision. The TISS model recognises the practitioner as an equal member within their own TISS team with the ability to define goals and design the steps to achieve those goals. Power constructs and how they may impede a practitioner's ability to fully participate in their own TISS team need to be kept on the TISS team's agenda and reviewed regularly.

The fifth principle, **empowerment, voice and choice**, relates to a practitioner's ability to be able to name what supports, including the type of supervision, they require to be able to effectively undertake their role. This may seem on the surface to be straightforward; however, practitioners are inducted into this vocation in a myriad of ways. Some of those ways may include hierarchical or toxic organisational cultures where supervision arrangements may have not been prioritised, been predominantly task-focused or where the supervisor was positioned as the expert and the practitioner as a passive receiver of supervision. A practitioner may never have had a 'good' supervision experience and therefore may not be able to name what it is that they need or what a responsive practitioner-centred arrangement might look like for them. Examples may have to be provided in some instances. Further, some practitioners may need to be supported to add or subtract supports as individual circumstances change.

The final principle, **cultural, historical and gender considerations**, in the context of the TISS model refers to sources of support where a practitioner may feel safest to fully engage with supervision. Examples could include a female identifying practitioner may wish to receive support from another female-identifying professional. This may be to reduce interruption from patriarchal oppression (real or perceived) and may create an opportunity for a practitioner to engage more fully with supports. Another example could be a practitioner's desire to engage in supports with another practitioner of the same cultural, language or religious background, again to remove barriers to participation and increase the effectiveness of supports.

## Revisiting the four core pillars central to the TISS model

The practitioner, the supervisor (and TISS team), the organisation and local contextualisation are the four pillars central to the TISS model. Working through these core pillars will form the basis of a practitioner's TISS plan. I will now summarise them.

**The practitioner**: Practitioners are at the centre of the TISS model. There would be no work with at-risk children and their families without them. Practitioners are central to ensuring the care and protection needs of vulnerable children are assessed and appropriately responded to. Elements to consider within this pillar are what one's motivation to undertake this work might be, what personal attributes one has that might require additional supports while working in a trauma-laden environment, for example. History of trauma, caring responsibilities, health status, etc., strategies that may have been successful previously to manage occupational traumatic stress, a thorough exploration of one's own existing skills, knowledge and qualifications are as well as professional interests, aspirations and what job satisfaction looks like.

**The supervisor (and the TISS team):** The supervisor pillar relates to the line supervisor within the TISS team. This is usually the person supervising the practitioner's work within their organisation. This pillar also relates to members of the TISS team which could include a paid external provider of supervision or a senior practitioner within the practitioner's organisation who does not have line supervision responsibilities, as examples. Similar to the practitioner pillar, line managers, supervisors and others involved in a practitioner's TISS team will also have a myriad of motivations for undertaking the role that they do in the context of working with vulnerable children and their families. As already outlined, transparency is a core principle informing the TISS model. Therefore, those participating in the model will need to thoroughly reflect on how much information about themselves they are willing to contribute. It is also important to have a frank and mature conversation about what a practitioner needs from their line supervisor and then to plan for the gaps to be filled by an alternative method of support.

**The organisation:** The organisation pillar relates to the organisation that a practitioner works for. It can also in some circumstances relate to the organisation, usually a government department, that funds the organisation or programme a practitioner works in. The inclusion of the examination of the organisational environment in which a practitioner works in a supervision context is unique to the TISS model. It is clear in the research literature, as discussed previously, that many organisations struggle to provide effective supervision to their workforce for a myriad of reasons. Some of those reasons include staff shortages, inability for an organisation to finance external supervision, organisational cultures that don't value or prioritise supervision, crisis-driven organisational environments where planning for such sessions can be difficult, and misalignment of professional backgrounds between practitioners and those supervising them. Acknowledging these shortcomings organisationally in the context of supervision will normalise these deficits and will provide practitioners with an opportunity to identify other sources of support that more adequately meet their individual needs. This is consistent with the second central acknowledgement of the TISS model, namely, that a practitioner's professional development and wellbeing support cannot be solely managed by their line supervisor.

**Local contextualisation:** The local contextualisation pillar relates to the place-based considerations that exist within the physical community that a practitioner is working in. Similar to the organisation pillar, the inclusion of the examination of the local community in which a practitioner works is unique to the TISS model. The size of the community, the socio/economic/political make-up of the community, access to universal services like health, housing and education, the settlement history, natural disaster or conflict history, and the dominant cultural background of the community will all impact practitioners working in those communities. Examining the benefits and challenges of living in the community a practitioner is working in, especially in the context of working with children at risk, is an important element of the TISS model. As an example, the smaller the community is in which a practitioner might work in, the more likely it is that they come into contact with children and families they have worked with outside of their work hours. Examples could include having children attend the same school, attending the same place of worship or participating in the same sporting or social group. There may be limited places to shop for essentials like groceries, medication or fuel. The smaller the community, the more a practitioner becomes visible which can lead to increased feelings of pressure and/or isolation. Understanding these elements and being able to analyse community issues from this framework is a strategy that will facilitate a practitioner's ability to externalise some of the occupational traumatic stress they may experience as a result of working with at-risk children and their families.

A TISS plan that has the four core pillars thoroughly examined will more likely suit the individual needs of the practitioner. Therefore, increasing capacity for effectiveness in supporting practitioners in their wellbeing and development requirements including working through experiences of occupational traumatic stress.

## Benefits of designing and implementing a TISS plan

I thought it might be useful to briefly explore the benefits of designing and implementing a TISS plan. There is no doubt that the preparation, design and implementation of a TISS plan is time-intensive. Traditional supervision models don't tend to have the same time investment in the design phase. Some traditional supervision models don't have a preparation or design phase, especially internal supervision provision. While there is a time component, engaging in the TISS model of support and supervision is an investment in the wellbeing and professional development of practitioners working with at-risk children and their families. Revisiting the first of the central acknowledgements, namely, the experience of occupational trauma is an occupational inevitability, it is crucial to have appropriate and effective supports in place for when practitioners start to experience occupational traumatic stress symptomologies. A TISS plan, including the preparation phase, can be a useful support system that facilitates preventative measures as well as a guide to managing symptomology post-exposure or at the onset of symptoms.

As already identified, there is a strong link in the research literature between the quality of the supervisory relationship, including the ability to establish and maintain trust, and practitioner's feeling supported in the work that they do with at-risk children and their families. However, in a practice sector with high staff turnover rates including practitioner turnover within line management roles, establishing long-standing relationships built on trust can be difficult to achieve. This is a core reason that I designed the TISS model as a team model. The TISS team model is informed by the second central acknowledgement, namely, a practitioner's professional development and wellbeing support cannot be solely managed by their line supervisor or manager. For example, if a practitioner is new to a team and has not yet established a relationship with their supervisor characterised by a sense of trust and safety, this element could be secured in another way, by another professional in the TISS team like an external supervisor or a peer support arrangement. A team approach to a practitioner's development and wellbeing needs also addresses several barriers identified in the research literature that impact a practitioner's ability to seek assistance when they start to experience occupational traumatic stress symptomology.

A team approach can also be beneficial in supporting the often unsupported wellbeing and development needs of line supervisors and managers. An example might be that if a line supervisor or manager begins to struggle with symptoms of occupational traumatic stress and they need additional time in their workday to resolve that symptomology, they can do so without the added burden of feeling they are not supporting their team appropriately. They may be able to delegate elements of a practitioner's wellbeing and development needs to another member of a practitioners TISS team temporarily. A team approach allows for such flexibility. A team approach informed by the three central acknowledgements that underpin the TISS model can facilitate professionally mature conversations that acknowledge occupational traumatic stress as an occupational inevitability. The acknowledgement can then provide organisations the opportunity to proactively plan for times when staff may be impacted by occupational traumatic stress symptomology, avoiding the situation where practitioners don't receive adequate support when their line supervisors and managers might be struggling themselves.

## Designing your own TISS plan

Now that the three central acknowledgements, six trauma-informed principles, the four core pillars and the benefits of implementing a professional wellbeing and development model like the TISS model have been revisited, I will now discuss how practitioners could go about designing and implementing their own TISS plan tailored to their own occupational context. There are three supporting documents to assist practitioners in developing and implementing their own TISS plan. These supporting documents are the TISS preparation worksheet, the TISS team agreement and the TISS plan. The generic documents are located in the Appendix section of this book. These documents were developed as a guide. Individuals and organisations are encouraged to individualise TISS agreements and plans to suit their circumstances and needs. I will now outline what the documents could be used for.

## The TISS preparation worksheet

The TISS preparation worksheet, located in the Appendix section of this book, was designed for practitioners wishing to design their own TISS plan to consider how the six trauma-informed principles and the four central pillars that underpin the TISS model could be applied to their own individual context. Also included in the TISS preparation worksheet are summarised definitions of the six trauma-informed principles and the four central pillars.

## The TISS team agreement document

As previously outlined, a practitioner's TISS team usually consists of a practitioner's line supervisor or manager, as well as other professionals who also have roles in providing wellbeing and development support. These other professionals may include a professional external supervisor, peers that participate in a peer support arrangement outlined in a practitioner's TISS plan, or others that provide other types of support like cultural, religious or spiritual supports. The TISS team agreement is a document that outlines who is involved in a practitioner's TISS plan and what their role is. TISS team agreements can also include things like an overall support statement, frequency of sessions, a communication agreement outlining expectations, how issues or disputes are to be managed, resources required to meet plan goals and review dates. I will briefly explore what these elements in the context of the TISS model might look like in practice.

**Line supervisor's name and core role**: Include name and role within the TISS team as well as what their role is in relation to the practitioner. This may seem fairly straightforward; however, it is important to explicitly outline what is the role of the line supervisor or manager and what is not. For example, a line supervisor or manager is not a therapist and therefore if there is a need for therapeutic support, this can be provided by another member of a practitioner's TISS team. Additionally, there may be some non-negotiable responsibilities that the line supervisor or manager cannot outsource to another member of the TISS team. An example of this might be matters pertaining to performance management or workload allocations.

**Other/s in the TISS team and their role**: Include name/s and role within the TISS team including frequency of sessions, if the sessions will occur during work time and a generic statement about the kind of support they are providing as part of the TISS plan. An example might be for a professional external supervisor – their role might be to explore the personal impacts of working with at-risk children and their families on the practitioner. This is a generic statement, however, it covers that the external supervisor will explore these issues including any elements of a practitioner's own experiences, in a private, confidential setting. This will also let the line supervisor or manager know that this element of a practitioner's overall wellbeing and development needs is being met outside of their supervisory remit.

**Support statement**: A support statement should reflect the TISS team's commitment to the practitioner at the centre of the TISS plan as well as a commitment to the model of support. One could add in here inherent practice values or something similar if appropriate.

**Frequency**: Frequency should include sessions between a practitioner and their line supervisor or manager as well as the frequency of engagements with others in the TISS plan like an external supervisor, community of practice group, and peer supports. Also included in this section should be what needs to happen if a session has to be cancelled or rescheduled.

**Communication agreement:** A communication agreement should be developed between all members of the TISS team. Consider what kinds of information should be shared between members. An example might be what kind of information should be shared between an external supervisor and an internal line supervisor about matters discussed by practitioners in sessions, if any at all. An example might be what the process and expectations would be if a practitioner discloses in an external supervision setting that they have been experiencing declining mental health that is impacting their work performance due to pressures being experienced in the workplace. Is there an expectation to inform the line supervisor or manager? Should that information remain confidential between the practitioner and their external supervisor? Whatever the TISS team (including the practitioner) agrees on, it should be explicit in the TISS team agreement. Additionally, consider how best to manage issues or disputes that may arise between members of the TISS team including the practitioner. Where will information about sessions be recorded, and who will have access within the TISS team? How should feedback be given, etc. The purpose of the communication agreement in the TISS team agreement is to make it explicit what will happen and why, in what circumstances and how this will be communicated.

**Resource allocation**: include costs of external providers as well as other professional development opportunities like training, conferences or journal subscriptions if they are identified in a practitioner's TISS plan. It is also important to outline the kind of costs. An example might be if sessions are to be attended during work hours, etc. How will additional costs be met? Will they be met by a practitioner's organisation or by the practitioner themselves? These expectations should also be explicitly outlined.

**Review date**: informed by the third central acknowledgement, namely, a practitioner's professional support needs will change over time, TISS team agreements and plan reviews should be scheduled on a regular and recurring basis. Review periods should be discussed and agreed upon mutually, as should the conditions that would necessitate an earlier review, like a role change, illness or a performance issue.

The generic proforma for the TISS team agreement is located in the Appendix section of this book.

## The TISS plan document

When completing the TISS plan document, it is important to have all the planning information including the notes from the reflective activities in previous chapters in mind. This is how a practitioner will design a TISS plan that is individualised to their own needs. The TISS plan document is designed to be short and succinct. It is not a reflection of how much preparation work went into its development. The preparation phase of TISS planning is for the practitioner to be able to identify what their individual needs are with their own occupational context. This places them in a better position to clearly articulate what their needs are and what the plan is to have those needs met.

TISS plans should include professional development needs of the practitioner, wellbeing needs, organisational needs and expectations, the administrative component, practitioner expectations of the line supervisor or manager (and other TISS team members), line supervisor or manager expectations of the practitioner and a review schedule. I will briefly explore what these elements in the context of the TISS model might look like in practice.

**Professional development needs:** This section pertains to the professional education and development needs of practitioners. Items might include upcoming training, formal mentoring arrangements with line supervisors or other colleagues, journal subscriptions or access to a professional library. This would also be the section to discuss levels of job satisfaction including what constitutes job satisfaction for that practitioner as well as professional aspirations including how a practitioner may work towards achieving those aspirations.

**Wellbeing needs:** The wellbeing section is where a practitioner outlines what their needs are in relation to maintaining their wellbeing in the workplace. Information from the TISS preparation worksheet should be included here. A practitioner's explicit personal needs don't need to be outlined here; however, the strategies and resources to meet those needs should be. For example, external supervision to assist in processing the personal history of domestic violence due to the amount of domestic violence present within the families that a practitioner is working with is not necessary. Including regular external supervision for matters pertaining to wellbeing is more than adequate.

**Organisational needs:** This section should include things like workload allocation, case reviews, outputs, case plan completion rates, mandatory training requirements, etc. This is also the section to discuss current organisational demands like staffing rates, current key organisational foci, upcoming changes in policies, procedures, or practices.

**Administration:** The administration section is where things like leave applications, issues pertaining to salary, timesheets, and employment conditions are discussed.

**Expectations of the practitioner:** This is the section where practitioners should explicitly outline what their expectations of their line supervisor or manager are. Items that may be included here are frequency of supervision, protocols around cancelling or rescheduling sessions, behaviour that demonstrates an interest in the practitioner's professional development and wellbeing, how feedback is preferred to be given, the process to raise issues or concerns, reasonable timeframes to receive responses to requests, etc. This section should be included in the TISS preparation document.

**Expectations of the supervisor:** This section is where the line supervisor or manager outlines their expectations of the practitioner including similar items to the practitioner section listed earlier.

**Expectations of others involved:** This section may not be included in all instances; however, it would include expectations pertaining to other members of the TISS team, such as an external supervisor. An external supervisor may include expectations like cancellation policies, payments, scheduling, and information exchange. A reference to the TISS team agreement document could also suffice here.

**Review schedule:** Like the TISS team agreement document, the review schedule is informed by the third central acknowledgement, namely, a practitioner's professional support needs will change over time. TISS team agreements and plan reviews should be scheduled on a regular and recurring basis. Similar to above, review periods should be discussed and agreed upon mutually, as should the conditions that would necessitate an earlier review like a role change, illness, or a performance issue.

## Tips for design and implementation

The most important thing to remember while designing a TISS plan is that the practitioner must be central to the exercise. That means that whatever goes in the TISS plan must be there as an element that supports the practitioner to have their wellbeing and development needs met. How that occurs is individual to each practitioner. The TISS model must be considered in its entirety – all the elements are evidence-based and work together to provide a framework of support for practitioners working in trauma-laden environments with at-risk children and their families.

## Chapter summary

In this chapter, creating and implementing a TISS plan including the central elements of the TISS model were revisited. Those elements being the three central acknowledgements, namely, the experience of occupational trauma is an occupational inevitability; a practitioner's professional development and wellbeing support cannot be solely managed by their line supervisor or manager; and a practitioner's professional support needs will change over time; the six trauma informed principles, namely, safety; trustworthiness and transparency; peer support, collaboration and mutuality; empowerment, voice and choice; and cultural, historical and gender considerations; and the four core pillars, namely, the practitioner, the supervisor (and TISS team), the organisation and local contextualisation. The supporting documents were outlined, namely, the TISS preparation worksheet, the TISS team agreement and the TISS plan. Tips to assist practitioners with preparing for, designing, implementing and reviewing their own TISS plans were also included.

## References

Beddoe, L., & Davys, A. (2016). *Challenges in professional supervision: Current themes and models for practice*. London: Jessica Kingsley Publishers.

Beddoe, L., Davys, A., & Adamson, C. (2014). "Never trust anybody who says 'I don't need supervision'": Practitioners beliefs about social worker resilience. *Practice (Birmingham, England)*, *26*(2), 113–130. https://doi.org/10.1080/09503153.2014.896888

Berger, R., & Quiros, L. (2016). Best practices for training trauma-informed practitioners: Supervisors' voice. *Traumatology*, *22*(2), 145–154. https://doi.org/10.1037/trm0000076

Hunt, S., Goddard, C., Cooper, J., Littlechild, B., & Wild, J. (2016). "If I feel like this, how does the child feel?" Child protection workers, supervision, management and organisational responses to parental violence. *Journal of Social Work Practice*, *30*(1), 5–24. https://doi.org/10.1080/02650533.2015.1073145

Kruzich, J., Mienko, J., & Courtney, M. (2014). Individual and work group influences on turnover intention among public child welfare workers: The effects of work group psychological safety. *Children and Youth Services Review*, *42*, 20–27. https://doi.org/10.1016/j.childyouth.2014.03.005

Little, M., Baker, T., & Jinks, A. (2018). A qualitative evaluation of community nurses' experiences of child safeguarding supervision. *Child Abuse Review*, *27*(2), 150–157. http://dx.doi.org/10.1002/car.2493

McCrae, J., Scannapieco, M., & Obermann, A. (2015). Retention and job satisfaction of child welfare supervisors. *Children and Youth Services Review*, *59*, 171–176. https://doi.org/10.1016/j.childyouth.2015.11.011

McFadden, P. (2020). Two sides of one coin? Relationships build resilience or contribute to burnout in child protection social work: Shared perspectives from leavers and stayers in Northern Ireland. *International Social Work*, *63*(2), 164–176. https://doi.org/10.1177/0020872818788393

Oates, F. (2019). You are not allowed to tell: Organisational culture as a barrier for child protection workers seeking assistance for traumatic stress symptomology. *Children Australia*, *44*(2), 84–90. https://doi.org/10.1017/cha.2019.12

Radey, M., & Stanley, L. (2018). "Hands on" versus "empty": Supervision experiences of frontline child welfare workers. *Children and Youth Services Review*, *91*, 128–136. https://doi.org/10.1016/j.childyouth.2018.05.037

Regehr, C. (2018). *Stress, trauma, and decision-making for social workers*. New York: Columbia University Press.

Substance Abuse and Mental Health Services Administration. (2014). *SAMHSA's concept of trauma and guidance for a trauma informed approach*. Rockville, MD: Substance Abuse and Mental Health Services Administration.

# Appendices

# Appendix 1.1

## TISS preparation worksheet

**Instructions:** This worksheet is designed for practitioners to use in preparation for the development of their TISS plan. Below the template are the definitions informing both the trauma-informed principles and the core pillars in the context of the TISS framework for reference.

Date: ____________________________________________

Practitioner name: ______________________________________

Practitioner role: _______________________________________

Current qualifications: ___________________________________

Professional experience: __________________________________

_________________________________________________________

_________________________________________________________

### Trauma-informed principles

As outlined throughout the book, the TISS model is informed by the six trauma-informed principles. Below is a table where you can write notes again each of the principles – this will assist you to identify what is important to include in your own TISS plan. Summarised definitions of the six trauma-informed principles in the context of the TISS model are located towards the end of this document under the subheading TISS preparation worksheet definitions.

| *Trauma-informed principles* | *Examples of how I can be supported in my role* |
|---|---|
| Safety | |
| Trustworthiness and transparency | |
| Peer support | |
| Collaboration and mutuality | |
| Empowerment, voice and choice | |
| Cultural, historical and gender considerations | |

## Four core pillars

The four core pillars central to the TISS model are the practitioner, the supervisor (and TISS team), the organisation; and local contextualisation. Think about what elements under each pillar you would include in your own TISS plan so that it individualised to your needs. Summarised definitions of the four core pillars in the context of the TISS model are located towards the end of this document under the subheading TISS preparation worksheet definitions.

| *Practitioner* | *Supervisor* | *Organisation* | *Local Contextualisation* |
|---|---|---|---|
| | | | |

## TISS preparation worksheet definitions

### *Trauma-informed principles*

Below are the trauma-informed principles that inform the TISS model. Please refer back to these when completing the preparation worksheet.

**Safety:** The safety principle applied within the TISS model context can refer to the practitioner's sense of safety within the supervisory relationship both perceived and in actual terms. The literature on practitioner experience of supervision has found that some practitioners avoid engaging in meaningful supervision due to a view that supervision is a tool used by their organisation to surveil them and their work. The safety principle can also underpin a practitioner's decision to share matters pertaining to their wellbeing.

**Trustworthiness and transparency:** The trustworthiness and transparency principle in the TISS model can refer to a shared sense of trust between a practitioner and their supervisor. As mentioned previously, the building and maintenance of trust in the supervisory relationship is critical and has been identified in the research literature as a key factor in a practitioner's ability to move through traumatic occupational experiences. The transparency part of this element should refer to transparency within the supervision process, that is, having clarity on the purpose of supervision, why certain matters are discussed and what the information will and will not be used for.

**Peer support:** The peer support principle in the TISS model context can relate to a practitioner's ability to include peer support in their support team. In practice, this could be the formal inclusion of a peer mentor where the purpose and scope are defined within the support team framework. Peer support could also be included in a non-formal capacity. Informal peer support could be included in a practitioner's support plan as a strategy for practitioners to utilise when they feel this kind of support would be beneficial, rather than in a prescribed schedule.

**Collaboration and mutuality:** The collaboration and mutuality can relate to the partnership element central to the TISS framework. The TISS framework holds the practitioner as an equal member within their own support team with the ability to define goals and design the steps to achieve those goals. Power constructs and how they may impede on a practitioner's ability to fully participate in their own TISS team need to be kept on the TISS team's agenda and reviewed regularly.

**Empowerment, voice, and choice:** The empowerment, voice, and choice principle in the context of the TISS model relates to a practitioner's ability to be able to name what supports they require to be able to effectively undertake their duties. Practitioners may need to be empowered to be able to voice what they need. TISS teams may need to provide examples of what more experienced practitioners have included in their support plans so that visualising what their needs might be can become clearer. This element has a strong emphasis on the integration of lived experience. In the context of the TISS model, integration of lived experience present within this principle refers to the lived experience of the practitioner themselves, which should always strongly inform individualised supervision and support plans. Practitioners need to be supported to add or subtract supports as individual circumstances change.

**Cultural, historical, and gender considerations:** The cultural, historical, and gender considerations principle in the context of the TISS model can refer to the inclusion of sources of support that a practitioner identifies with. As an example, a female-identifying practitioner may wish to receive support from other female-identifying professionals. This may be to reduce interruption from patriarchal oppression (real or perceived) and create an opportunity for a practitioner to engage more fully with their supports. Similarly, a practitioner may wish to engage in supports with another practitioner of the same cultural or language background, again to remove barriers to participation and increase the effectiveness of support. I have shared throughout the book my own research findings relating to the support and supervision needs of First Nation's practitioners who work with vulnerable children and their families. A key learning from this research is not to assume what the support needs of First Nation practitioners might be, given the negative historical and current experiences of First Nation communities have had with child protection authorities. The needs of the practitioner are central in the application of the TISS model. Autonomy over voicing individual needs is paramount, and assumptions should not be made by line supervisors or managers about what support might best suit individual practitioners.

## Four core pillars

There are four pillars that support the TISS framework. They are the practitioner, the supervisor, the organisation and local contextualisation. The four pillars within the TISS framework are further defined below. Please refer to them when completing this worksheet.

**Practitioners:** Practitioners are at the centre of the TISS model. Practitioners come to this kind of work for a myriad of reasons including that they themselves may have experienced similar trauma to the vulnerable children and their families that they work with. Vulnerable children and their families need healthy and grounded professionals to assist them in navigating through their own trauma and related situational crisis and into a space where children can have their care and protection needs met adequately. Practitioners need to be engaged in conversations about their motivations to undertake this kind of work. Within an individual's motivations will be clues that inform what kinds of supports may assist them when they start to inevitably experience the effects of occupational traumatic stress. Anchoring practitioners to the core reasons they chose to undertake work with vulnerable children and their families can be a strategy to move practitioners through their experience of occupational traumatic stress back to a place of internal safety. It may be useful for practitioners to explore what their triggers might be and how they have successfully navigated distressing experiences in the past. It must be acknowledged that there may be ethical considerations about whether or not it is appropriate for a practitioner's line supervisor or manager to engage practitioners in these kinds of conversations. These explorations may be better undertaken between a practitioner and an external supervisor so that the practitioner's knowledge about what their professional support needs might be, without the threat (real or perceived) of such information being used for purposes it wasn't intended to be used for, later, like performance management or other matters related to a practitioner's conduct.

Another element central to the practitioner pillar is to thoroughly explore the professional background of a practitioner. Many practitioners will come to their roles with varied professional experience including skills, knowledge and professional interests. Again, these elements of a practitioner's background may give insights into how best to move practitioners through occupational traumatic stress, increasing their feelings of job satisfaction and intention to remain in their position.

It is always preferred to explore these elements in times when a practitioner is not experiencing acute occupational traumatic stress. While setting up a successful TISS plan in line with the TISS model can be resource-intensive in the beginning, having these elements established at the beginning of a professional relationship will create less stress for all involved later.

**TISS team – line supervisors and others:** the role of line supervisors, managers and other professional supports are key in the context of the TISS model. Similar to the practitioner pillar, line managers, supervisors and others involved in a practitioner's TISS team will also have a myriad of motivations for undertaking the role that they do in the context of working with vulnerable children and their families. As already outlined, transparency is a core principle in the TISS model. Therefore, those participating in the model will need to thoroughly reflect on how much information about themselves they are willing to contribute. There is power in expressing vulnerability to those one supervises especially in relation to motivations for undertaking the work and the strategies one may have used previously to move through the experience of occupational traumatic stress. However, drawing on the work of George Kohlrieser on secure base leadership outlined in the previous chapter, leaders who operate from an internal state of safety are the most effective in guiding practitioners through occupational traumatic stress. Another key principle of the TISS model is critical reflection. It is this principle that calls on all practitioners who make up a TISS team to critically reflect on their own histories of trauma, including their experience of occupational trauma, and to establish where their boundaries are in the context of working within the TISS framework. Protective professional boundaries do not exclude line supervisors, managers, and others from participating within the TISS framework. As already outlined, a central acknowledgement underpinning the TISS model is that a practitioner's professional development and wellbeing support cannot be provided by one source. Therefore, if a practitioner feels that their professional development and wellbeing support would benefit from engagement with a professional who at that point in time would be comfortable using their lived experience as a support strategy, then the TISS model allows for this. A team approach to supporting practitioners who work with vulnerable children and their families facilitates the opportunity for practitioners to receive the support they require without compromising the boundaries of line supervisors and managers.

**Organisation:** Already established in this book is the struggle organisations have had, and continue to have, in providing adequate support and supervision to practitioners who meet their needs. I am not of the view that organisations set out with an explicit agenda to fail their practitioners in this regard. As discussed in this book, organisations struggle to provide effective and responsive support to practitioners for a myriad of complex and intersecting reasons. Acknowledging with practitioners where they are located within a larger system can assist practitioners in working through occupational distress that is rooted in a systemic context. An example of this might be when practitioners develop a sense of hopelessness working within the 'system'. In my own time working with practitioners, it is almost always the 'system' that contributes to a practitioner's decision to leave their role working with vulnerable children and their families rather than the vulnerable children and families themselves. Internalised hopelessness and the feeling that the work practitioners do is meaningless can be overwhelming. This paralysis can lead to practitioners not fully engaging in their work or monitoring their own wellbeing. When a practitioner has a solid understanding of the 'system' in which they work including from a sociological, political and cultural viewpoint, they are in a better professional position to navigate that system and to broker better outcomes for the vulnerable children and their families that they work with. Supporting practitioners to externalise their feelings of hopelessness is an effective strategy for line supervisors and managers attempting to move practitioners through identified occupational traumatic stress.

The TISS model seeks to acknowledge the inherent complexities, including structural, that come with working with vulnerable children and their families. The TISS model seeks to identify these complexities so that mitigation strategies can be included within a practitioner's TISS plan. An example of this might be acknowledging organisational complexities pertaining to practitioner workloads. In most jurisdictions and practice settings, there are policy and procedural guides outlining expectations in relation to workload especially when it comes to the number of cases an individual practitioner may have responsibility for. However, anyone who has worked in a child welfare organisation knows that there can be a chasm between ideal workloads and the reality. Child welfare organisations are plagued by high staff turnover rates and difficulty recruiting and retaining experienced practitioners especially in rural and remote communities. High turnover rates contribute to high workloads for the remaining practitioners and their line supervisors and managers. These complexities are reported consistently in the research literature across jurisdictions (Hunt et al., 2016; Oates, 2019). Given the research literature, one can accurately conclude that unreasonable workloads within a child welfare organisational context do significantly negatively impact the wellbeing of practitioners and needs to be acknowledged within TISS plans. The power of acknowledgement cannot be underestimated. It will give practitioners the safety to raise issues pertaining to workload without the fear of being deemed as not suitable for the position if they cannot keep up with the workload. Strategies may include that workload is added as a standing agenda item in TISS plans and that purposeful, targeted discussions pertaining to workloads occur regularly.

**Local contextualisation:** Implementing the TISS model without due consideration of matters pertaining to local contextualisation would likely result in less effective results for practitioners. Any practitioner who has worked with vulnerable children and their families in a rural or remote community or in a community where the dominant culture is not their own, will already has an innate understanding of why incorporating local contextualisation into a practitioner's TISS plan is critically important. Having a good understanding of the sociological, economic and political factors that impact communities is invaluable information for practitioners to acquire. Understanding these elements and being able to analyse community issues from this framework is a strategy that will facilitate a practitioner's ability to externalise some of the occupational traumatic stress they may experience as a result of working with vulnerable children and their families. There are complex reasons, far bigger than any one individual practitioner, that contribute to children experiencing abuse and neglect. Having said that, practitioners still have a responsibility to undertake professional learning and development to ensure that they have contemporary knowledge and skills to assist families and communities to best meet the care and protective needs of their children. This is a balance that requires ongoing analysis and evaluation within a supervision context. Questions that a practitioner and their supports may ask themselves within a local contextualisation context might include:

- What is the history of the community we work in? Does the community have a history of traumatic events like ongoing military conflict, natural disasters, dispossession of land due to colonisation or high rates of humanitarian settlement?
- What is the demographic landscape of the community? Does the community have a lot of older people in comparison to younger people and families for example? Are there large numbers of migrant or newly arrived people who don't have English as a first language?
- What socioeconomic factors impact the community? Is the community deemed to be predominantly lower socioeconomic in categorisation? What are the unemployment rates? Is there adequate access to housing, education, healthcare and other social support services? Is there an above-average incarceration rate?

Another element of the local contextualisation pillar within the TISS model that requires addressing is how living in the community a practitioner works in impacts them or could potentially impact them. The nature of the work means that working with people who are hostile towards practitioners in this field is enviable. As an example, the smaller the community you work in, the more likely it will be that practitioners are interacting with the vulnerable children and families they work with outside of their regular work hours. Examples of this include attending the same church or social group, having children that attend the same school, being in the same friendship group or being on the same sports team. There may only be a handful of shops where you can purchase groceries, fuel, or other essentials. The smaller the community, the more a practitioner's visibility increases. This can lead to practitioners feeling they have to alter how they would normally spend their time outside of work, where they would go or who they would interact with. Practitioners in my own research stated that they had increased visibility within the community in which they worked due to their Indigeneity, which brings with it a number of complexities. Increased visibility, in general, can contribute to practitioners not being able to have restful breaks from their work. The other element to keep in mind in the context of this pillar is that the smaller the community, the less access practitioners will have to professionals who may support them with their own issues pertaining to wellbeing. Practitioners may not be comfortable working with a psychologist, social worker or other therapeutic practitioner with whom they also interact on a professional level. This pillar advocates for other options to be canvassed like connecting with therapeutic support via phone or video sessions.

# Appendix 1.2

## TISS team agreement

**Instructions:** The TISS team agreement should include the date the agreement was made, a support statement that demonstrates the team's (including the practitioner's) commitment to the TISS process, name and roles of those in the team, the frequency of supports, a communication agreement including how issues or disputes are to be managed, the resource allocation required, the date of review and participant signatures.

Date: ____________________________________________

Support statement: ____________________________________________

Practitioner name & role: ____________________________________________

Supervisor: ____________________________________________

Other/s and their role: ____________________________________________

Frequency: ____________________________________________

Communication agreement: ____________________________________________

Resource allocation: ____________________________________________

Review date: ____________________________________________

Signatures: ____________________________________________

Below are some suggestions about how to complete the domains in the above proforma:

**Date:** Date the agreement is undertaken.

**Support statement**: A support statement should reflect the TISS team's commitment to the practitioner at the centre of the TISS plan as well as a commitment to the model of support. One could add in here inherent practice values or something similar if appropriate.

**Line supervisor's name and core role**: Include name and role within the TISS team as well as what their role is in relation to the practitioner. This may seem fairly straightforward; however, it is important to explicitly outline what is the role of the line supervisor or manager and what is not. For example, a line supervisor or manager is not a therapist and therefore if there is a need for therapeutic support, this can be provided by another member of a practitioner's TISS team. Additionally, there may be some non-negotiable responsibilities that the line supervisor or manager cannot outsource to another member of the TISS team. An example of this might be matters pertaining to performance management or workload allocations.

**Other/s and their role**: Include name/s and role within the TISS team including frequency of sessions, whether will they occur during work time, and a generic statement about the kind of support they are providing as part of the TISS plan. An example might be for a professional external supervisor – their role might be to explore the personal impacts of working with at-risk children and their families on the practitioner. This is a generic statement; however, it covers that the external supervisor will explore these issues including any elements of a practitioner's own experiences in a private confidential setting. This will also let the line supervisor or manager know that this element of a practitioner's overall wellbeing and development needs is being met outside of their supervisory remit.

**Frequency**: Frequency should include sessions between a practitioner and line supervisor as well as frequency of engagements with others in the TISS plan like an external supervisor, community of practice group, and peer supports. Also included in this section should be what should happen if a session needs to be cancelled or rescheduled.

**Communication agreement:** A communication agreement should be developed between all members of the TISS team. Consider what kinds of information should be shared between members. An example might be what kind of information should be shared between an external supervisor and an internal line supervisor about matters discussed by practitioners in sessions, if any at all. An example might be what the process and expectations would be if a practitioner discloses in an external supervision setting that they have been experiencing thoughts of harming themselves due to pressures being experienced in the workplace. Is there an expectation to inform the line supervisor or manager? Should that information remain confidential between the practitioner and their external supervisor? Whatever the TISS team (including the practitioner) agrees on, it should be explicit in the TISS team agreement. Additionally, consider how best to manage issues or disputes that may arise between members of the TISS team including the practitioner. Where will information about sessions be recorded, and who will have access within the TISS team? How should feedback be given, etc.? The purpose of the communication agreement in the TISS team agreement is to make it explicit what will happen and why under what circumstances, and how this will be communicated.

**Resource allocation**: Include costs of external providers, journal subscriptions if identified as a professional development tool, etc. It is also important to outline in-kind costs like if sessions are to be attended during work hours, etc. How will additional costs be met, for example, organisationally or by the practitioner, should also be explicitly outlined.

**Review date**: Informed by the third central acknowledgement, namely, a practitioner's professional support needs will change over time, TISS team agreements and plans reviews should be scheduled on a regular and recurring basis. Review periods should be discussed and agreed upon mutually, as should the conditions that would necessitate an earlier review like a role change, illness, or a performance issue.

# Appendix 1.3

## TISS plan

**Instructions:** This example TISS plan is to give practitioners, supervisors, and others an idea of what should be included in a TISS plan. Individuals and organisations are encouraged to develop their own proforma documents to suit their operational needs. Information from the preparation worksheet should be included in the TISS plan. This TISS framework should be at the forefront of mind when completing the TISS plan.

Date: ______________________________

Practitioner name & role: ______________________________

Supervisor: ______________________________

Other/s and their role: ______________________________

Current qualifications: ______________________________

Professional experience: ______________________________
______________________________

Review date: ______________________________

Signatures: ______________________________

Below are some suggestions about how to complete the domains in the above proforma:

**Professional development needs:** This section pertains to the professional education and development needs of practitioners. Items might include upcoming training, formal mentoring arrangements with line supervisors or other colleagues, journal subscriptions or access to a professional library. This would also be the section to discuss levels of job satisfaction including what constitutes job satisfaction for that practitioner as well as professional aspirations including how a practitioner may work towards achieving those aspirations.

**Wellbeing needs:** The wellbeing section is where a practitioner outlines what their needs are in relation to maintaining their wellbeing in the workplace. Information from the TISS preparation worksheet should be included here. A practitioner's explicit personal needs don't need to be outlined here, however, the strategies and resources to meet those needs should be. For example, regular external supervision for matters pertaining to wellbeing rather than external supervision to assist processing personal history of domestic violence due to amount of domestic violence present within the families that a practitioner is working with is adequate.

**Organisational needs:** This section should include things like workload allocation, case reviews, outputs, case plan completion rates, and mandatory training requirements. This is also the section to discuss current organisational demands like staffing rates, current key organisational foci, and upcoming changes in policies, procedures, or practices.

**Administration:** The administration section is where things like leave applications, issues pertaining to salary, timesheets, and employment conditions are discussed.

**Expectations of the practitioner:** This is the section where practitioners should explicitly outline what their expectations of their line supervisor are. Items that may be included here are frequency of supervision, protocols around cancelling or rescheduling sessions, behaviour that demonstrates an interest in the practitioner's professional development and wellbeing, how feedback is preferred to be given, the process to raise issues or concerns, reasonable timeframes to receive responses to requests, etc. This section should be informed by the TISS preparation document.

**Expectations of the supervisor:** This section is where the line supervisor or manager outlines their expectations of the practitioner including similar items to the practitioner.

**Expectations of others involved:** This section may not be included in all instances; however, it would include expectations pertaining to other members of the TISS team, such as an external supervisor. An external supervisor may include expectations like cancellation policies, payments, scheduling, and information exchange. A reference to the TISS team agreement document could also suffice here.

**Review schedule:** Similar to the TISS team agreement document, the review schedule is informed by the third central acknowledgement, namely, a practitioner's professional support needs will change over time; TISS team agreements and plans reviews should be scheduled on a regular and recurring basis. Review periods should be discussed and agreed upon mutually, as should the conditions that would necessitate an earlier review, like a role change, illness, or a performance issue.

## References

Hunt, S., Goddard, C., Cooper, J., Littlechild, B., & Wild, J. (2016). "If I feel like this, how does the child feel?" Child protection workers, supervision, management and organisational responses to parental violence. *Journal of Social Work Practice*, *30*(1), 5–24. https://doi.org/10.1080/02650533.2015.1073145

Oates, F. (2019). You are not allowed to tell: Organisational culture as a barrier for child protection workers seeking assistance for traumatic stress symptomology. *Children Australia*, *44*(2), 84–90. https://doi.org/10.1017/cha.2019.12

# Index